D0757816

To ANN,

Surfing the rift

My big sister
and a true
artist in
every way !
Love
Joe

Surfing the rift

*The Executive's Guide to the
Post-Web 2.0 World*

Dr. Tanuja Singh and Joe Cullinane

© 2009 by Cullinane Media.

Library of Congress Control Number: 2009908966
ISBN: Hardcover   978-1-4415-7070-3
               Softcover   978-1-4415-7069-7

All rights reserved. No part of this book may be reproduced or transmitted in any form
or by any means, electronic or mechanical, including photocopying, recording, or by
any information storage and retrieval system, without permission in writing from the
copyright owner.

This book was printed in the United States of America.

To order additional copies of this book, contact:
Xlibris Corporation
1-888-795-4274
www.Xlibris.com
Orders@Xlibris.com
59121

Contents

Dedications from the authors

This book is dedicated to my parents, Krishna Kant Pant and Hemlata Pant, who instilled in me a lifelong love for learning. And, to Charles Cullinane. Thanks Dad. It's been 25 years, and I still miss you.

Acknowledgements

We are grateful for the encouragement and support given us by so many friends, business associates, and family members during the writing of this book.

Our family members: Vinisha Joshi, Gaurav Pant and Jasvinder Singh, Marianne Cullinane, Charlie Cullinane, Charles Cullinane and Mike Cullinane. Our students in the following classes at Northern Illinois University provided insight and challenge: Marketing and New Technology, Spring 2008; Global Marketing Management; Principles of Global Marketing class, Fall 2008; Integrated Marketing Communications; and the NIU Experiential Learning Center's Barsema microfinance team; Cullinane media team; and McDonald's team. A special note of appreciation to: Sandi Byrd, Scott Carlson, Aline Click, Danny Crescent, Tim Draper, Diane Dunne, Bob Drake, Rebecca Gorshe, Dan Heiser, Kristen Highland, Tony Hsieh, Jessica Jackley, Steven Jones, Alison Kuczwara, Aaron Magness, Jane Mall, Mig Pascual, Sarah Pearson, Emily Reed, Lindsey Savoie, Denise Schoenbachler, Kraig Smith, Mark Smith, Nick Ustanko, Laura Vasquez and Carl Volk.

The authors

Dr. Tanuja Singh is the Dean of the Bill Greehey School of Business at St. Mary's University in San Antonio, TX. An award-winning educator, she has published extensively in acclaimed academic and trade journals, and presented at several national and international conferences. Her research, teaching, and consulting interests include digital media and its impact on businesses and people; global and cross-cultural marketing; and public policy issues in marketing. She has worked in international banking specializing in export-import trade and served as a consultant to several private and public sector organizations, including *Fortune 500* companies. Dr. Singh has more than fifteen years of experience teaching executives; graduate and undergraduate students; and has conducted many management workshops and seminars in the U.S., Egypt, India, China, and South Korea among others. She earned a doctorate in business administration with a specialization in marketing from Southern Illinois University at Carbondale; an M.B.A. from Millsaps College in Jackson, MS; and an M.S. in Physics from India's Allahabad University. She was department chair in the department of marketing at Northern Illinois University in DeKalb, prior to joining the Greehey School of Business in July 2009.

Joe Cullinane, based in California's Silicon Valley, is an advisor, consultant, educator, author, and speaker who counsels executives and entrepreneurs on best practices to achieve their business goals. His areas of expertise include strategic business development; global sales and marketing; and the strategic deployment of Internet technologies in support of business development and branding initiatives. Cullinane is the author of *21st Century Selling: An Anthology of Advice from Top Sales Pros*. Cullinane learned first-hand the power of strategic business development and brand marketing in positions with Xerox Corporation and NCR Corporation. At Diversified Software Systems,

Inc., a leading enterprise software company, he served as Vice President of Business Development; Vice President of Marketing; Vice President of International Sales; and Western Region Sales Manager; conducting business and delivering training on five continents. At Northern Illinois University's College of Business, Cullinane was an executive-in-residence and taught courses in global marketing, marketing, technology, and entrepreneurship. He coached student teams in the NIU Experiential Learning Center and also taught sales and marketing courses at the Keller Graduate School of Management and Aurora University. Cullinane earned an M.S.C. in managerial communications from Northwestern University, M.B.A. from Dominican University, and B.S. in marketing from Northern Illinois University. In 2005, Cullinane received the annual Outstanding Alumni Award from the NIU Department of Marketing.

Introduction

Welcome to the world of participant media where customers are in control—and where they can become some of your best marketers!

Surfing the rift provides a review of the technologies changing the face of business, and it offers suggestions for leveraging these technologies to your advantage. This guide covers a variety of new media and technologies, including blogs, podcasts, vlogs, social networks, virtual worlds, search engine optimization (SEO), search engine marketing (SEM), and business collaboration tools. It also helps you address some fundamental questions: Who are your customers; what types of relationships do they desire with you; and which technologies, strategies and tactics will keep you connected most effectively to your customers?

Why title it *Surfing the rift*? We've long accepted the metaphor of "surfing the net," acknowledging the Internet's nonlinear, hyperlinked structure that we can deftly navigate by browsing and searching to effortlessly ride the waves of readily accessible online information. *Surfing the rift* then suggests ways you can identify the rifts—or shifts—and how to use the right mix of technologies to glide over them safely without a wipe-out that could threaten the viability of your business.

For example, only a few years ago search engine optimization (SEO) was a relatively unknown concept but quickly became an important method for building visibility and brand awareness. Companies that were early adopters of SEO were able to gain a competitive advantage. SEO created a rift and those who surfed it successfully became market trendsetters. Depending on how you approach it, a rift can be an opportunity or a roadblock.

What's causing these rifts? And what should you be doing about it? We believe three factors have caused recent and significant rifts:

1. Generational differences in the adoption and use of technology
2. Rapid obsolescence of old paradigms such as interruption marketing
3. A cascade of new information technologies—broadly characterized as Web 2.0 or social media—that enable quickly evolving business strategies and interactive, engaging tactics

As an example of the first factor, consider the behaviors of Baby Boomers (born 1946-1964) and members of Generation Y (born 1982-1995). While Boomers began using LinkedIn as a professional networking platform, their younger counterparts eagerly adopted Facebook for both social and business networking. Over time, gaps in adoption and use inevitably narrow. Now the fastest growing segment embracing social networks such as Facebook are women over age 55.

It is said that the race goes to the swift, and we believe you can gain a competitive edge by identifying, understanding, and strategically employing new technologies ahead of your competitors. The main idea is to determine where your market is today, where it will be going tomorrow, and surf there first to catch the best waves.

You will find examples throughout the book of how old paradigms are being replaced by new media and technologies that connect marketers with consumers pre-disposed to their messages, products, and solutions. We show how participant media is about more than simply targeting—it's about targeting at the right moment and engaging with the right message in a wholly credible, user-driven, interactive environment. Marketing becomes a series of conversations among participating small groups of customers, influencers, and marketers, which is why we use the term **participant media** to describe new media/social media as it relates to marketing. We'll use the terms interchangeably to show you how to participate effectively in conversations for major impact and results.

The rapid adoption of participant media technologies—our third rift-creating factor—is evident in the quickly evolving Web blogosphere. As text blogs attained critical mass around 2004, along came podcasts to extend blogging into the realm of portable, downloadable, audio content. And, as podcasting was gathering momentum, Web-based video—most notably YouTube—roared onto the scene. Today, video and audio are staple components of popular blogs and Web sites in almost every category.

We wrote this book to give you the understanding and tools to convert these game-changing, technology-generated rifts into opportunities for success.

In California's Silicon Valley, the term "first mover" was coined to describe the first company to enter or create a market segment. You don't always want to be a "first mover" because if you are too far ahead of the curve it can get lonely (and unprofitable) waiting for a market to develop around an innovative idea. As in other aspects of life, timing is important. But knowing how to navigate the rifts by using social media technologies and platforms can give you just-in-time "first mover" status, when a head start of mere weeks or months or even five minutes can spell the difference between the leaders and the also-rans.

Surfing the rift will help you look at ways to leverage participant media in your marketplace. For, in addition to creating rifts in the business landscape, these media have spawned great opportunities for a new kind of relationship with customers and prospects that is more organic and that encourages sharing tools, messages and processes. Change is a constant in our business lives, and today's successful executive's best option for success in the new media world is learning to surf the rift ahead of the next wave.

So, are you ready to surf the rift? You soon will be! Read the following chapters to gain insight into the most popular and productive participant media tools and technologies.

Chapter 1

Shift happened! Hello participant media

Think about the amount of time you spend using technology to complete your everyday tasks. From booking concert and sports tickets to checking your flight status, where do you turn for information? How would your life change if the ubiquitous Internet shut down for even one day? How well could you function without your BlackBerry, GPS, e-mail or iPhone? Chances are your life—your business—would be disrupted in a major way if your supporting technologies did not function. Even in the world of politics and government, social media tools have a major role. Then-Senator Barack Obama used these tools to build a grassroots movement that helped get him elected U.S. president. During the recent crisis in Iran, the rest of the world was kept abreast through postings on Twitter, Facebook and YouTube. These technologies change not only your personal world, but the business and socio-political world, too, and they will play a major role in determining the mediascape for the next decade.

Let's begin with a simple exercise. What do you know about podcasts, blogs, RSS, social networks, avatars, wikis, and search engine marketing? Ever heard of LinkedIn or Viddler? How about Second Life?

Think that much of this is teenspeak and not critical to your company's bottom line? Think again! A McKinsey survey of marketing executives from a diverse group of global industries found most respondents acutely aware of the potential of these new technologies for business creation and growth. They reported an expected 10 percent or more sales growth from online channels by 2010, and these projections are determining where the industries will spend their money today.[1]

This book posits that there are three primary factors causing the shifts that are radically altering today's business and marketing environments: generational differences, media fragmentation and the adoption of bold new technologies that empower individuals. This book looks at the technologies propelling the shifts, and examines how these changes affect every firm and every individual. It also discusses what successful executives should know if they wish to remain informed and relevant in our globally connected and fast moving, technology-driven world.

We know that mass marketing is seldom used as the only and best method for reaching today's customers. Gone are the days of interruption marketing where firms large and small controlled the media and the message. We've shifted from mass marketing and interruption marketing, which marketers designed, managed and controlled, to marketing to individuals who generate and control customized messages. This shift in not merely the mediascape but in the mindset has created great opportunities for a new kind of relationship with the customer that is more organic, but one that is also risky if you cannot manage the tools, the messages, and the process. The question is: have you and your firm adapted to these changes, and more importantly, can you anticipate what's coming?

Another factor to consider is that members of Gen Y are entering the work force. There are 80 million of them, and they text each other on mobile phones; post and watch homemade videos on YouTube; and share personal information on Facebook. They are participating in and responding to a new communication model that smart marketers are leveraging. This book will help you understand this shift and the powerful potential of its enabling technologies. You'll find here an overview of the critical technologies changing the face of business, as well as suggestions for capitalizing on these technologies. You'll not only discover how successful companies prosper by adapting to these changes, but how you can succeed in this technology-dominated and customer-driven new world order where political and geographic boundaries have given way to cyber communities (and the operative word is community—even though it may exist only in cyberspace)!

Living in a LinkedIn world

Let's look at some numbers—more than 75 percent of the U.S. adult population now uses the Internet. By the time you read this, the number may have gone up again. Worldwide, between 2006 and 2011, a 38 percent increase is expected in the number of people with Internet access, which currently stands at about 1.2 billion people. These people are young, educated, more affluent than their non-Internet-using counterparts, and technology addicted. Among 18-29 year olds in the U.S., Internet usage is a whopping 92 percent and among those 30-49, it is a very respectable 85 percent. Among college graduates the use goes up to 93 percent, and for people who earn more than $50,000 a year, the usage is 90 percent.[2]

This trend not only signifies more people migrating to these technologies but also abandoning traditional media, and putting more faith in user-generated content. In this bold new world, peers serve as friends, philosophers, and confidants, and electronic word-of-mouth (e-WOM) has replaced company-generated content. Peer-to-peer networks dominate cyberspace and determine how to create, share, disseminate and use information. These changes are causing significant shifts—technology has gone from being a mere facilitator to being integral to our existence—and these shifts are changing everything from the nature of our work life to the very nature of our societies.

Technology dictates how firms manage everything from customer relationships to assets and information. A McKinsey report stated that slightly more than a third of the marketing executives polled from around the world noted that their companies frequently use digital advertising tools such as blogs, podcasts and many others.[3] In addition, smart phones let people carry the power of social computing wherever they go. An explosive proliferation of software applications—and easy ways to get them—is changing our relationship with mobile phones. The always-connected era is dawning. The cell phone is becoming more a companion than just a means for one-on-one conversation.[4]

From customer service to product development and market research, companies use a wide variety of tools that we'll explore, including wikis, blogs, search engine marketing, podcasts, videos, and virtual worlds. These new tools will continue to grow in prominence; companies must take notice because the shift has already happened!

What is happening to marketing?

> "The interruption-disruption model is dying out, thanks to shifting consumer trends. Consumers are increasingly in control of their media content and can easily eradicate ads they don't want to see." Geoff Ramsey, CEO, Emarketer[5]

From the 1920s and through the mid 1990s, the interruption model was the predominant model of mass media marketing. The implied contract was simply that the sponsor or advertiser paid for programming, and we agreed to watch their commercial messages. This model worked well as long as there was one television per family and the major networks controlled programming and timing. Now, the audience for marketing messages is fragmented and consumers are turning off and tuning out—or tuning on to participant media buzz and friends' opinions about products and events. Today's participant media engages and empowers individuals to freely share their ideas and experiences—your customers become some of your best spokespersons and marketers!

In the 21st century a number of factors are leading to a rethinking of this model.

- Over exposure: By some estimates the average consumer receives more than 3,000 marketing messages a day and well over 1,000,000 per year.[6] Not surprisingly, this level of exposure completely overwhelms our limited capacity for processing, given our time constraints and the inherent need to optimize our information consumption and usage.

- Irrelevance: A Yankelovich Partners study found that almost 60 percent of U.S. consumers consider marketing personally irrelevant. Perhaps even more importantly, almost 70 percent are interested in products and services that would help block marketing attempts. Somewhat ironically, the same study also found that customers respond more favorably to marketing messages when they have some control over what they see, when they see it, whether they can personalize it to fit their needs, and whether they can participate actively in the marketing process.[7] In essence, people may be more open to marketing messages when they can control the delivery and format, and when they find relevant, personal meaning in them.

- Annoyance factor: Not surprisingly, excessive exposure to irrelevant marketing messages annoys an audience. Nearly half of the customers in a recent study say the amount of marketing and advertising to which they are exposed detracts from their experience of everyday life.[8]

- Emergence of online communities: A 2006 study found that these same people spend 27 percent of their Internet usage time everyday engaged in online communities—the same amount of time they spend for entertainment but more than what they spend on gathering news or shopping![9] So, people don't mind distractions—as long as they are meaningful.

- New technologies and legislation. "Do-not-call" registries, TIVO, spam filters, pop-up blockers, and caller ID reveals add to the difficulty of marketing to buyers. Anti-spam, anti-adware, anti-telemarketing, and no-soliciting laws can block marketers from potential customers. However, when customers reach out to you by opting-in, they are already engaged and more likely to respond to your messages.

- Eroding trust: An evaluation of 4,000 product reviews found most buyers do not trust the marketing messages. Companies have not done enough to generate trust. However, consumers do trust user-generated content to provide them with useful information. Another study suggested that 36 percent of consumers are not just indifferent to marketing but they have a very negative view of marketing attempts. Only 24 percent believe marketers tell the truth in ads.[10] They trust other consumers and rely on e-WOM. The ties they create among themselves are strengthening even as trust in marketing and marketers continues to decline

- Attention span: The text messaging, multi-tasking generation does not want to watch a 30-second commercial. It has neither the time nor the inclination to passively receive advertiser-generated messages.[11]

The good news? Traditional media channels have lost their monopoly on reaching large audiences. David Neelman, former CEO of Jetblue Airways Corporation, posted videos directly to YouTube[12] and reached out to online communities frequented by his customers. Customers, vendors and other stakeholders have moved to new places, including social networks such as LinkedIn, Facebook and MySpace. They inhabit the virtual worlds of Second Life and There.com. They watch hulu.com, Viddler, and YouTube.

Steve Anderson in the *Automated Agency Report* notes quite candidly that "unless you are living in a cave, you can't help but notice the impact of, or at least the buzz about, social networking sites."[13] Customers are migrating in huge numbers to new participant media, which are always on and can be accessed on their own terms. They listen to podcasts, read and write blogs, watch online videos, and follow thought leaders of their own choosing on Twitter. At work they collaborate using wikis and cloud computing. People not only consume the new media and tools, but they participate in the conversation and ultimately create the content. They also create word-of-mouth buzz advertising and engage in brand building. In essence, consumers create and produce content, and link to other consumers around the world in ways unthinkable only a few years ago.

The new Internet: Web 2.0

The second generation of the Internet is commonly referred to as Web 2.0, which includes social media and user-generated content. The term Web 2.0 has become common parlance since Tim O'Reilly and Dale Dougherty coined it in 2004 to describe a set of principles and practices that include looking at the Web as a "platform" and "harnessing collective intelligence."[14] Web 1.0 is commonly used to define the first generation of one-way online communications, e.g. Yahoo news, in which the average online user could not readily participate. In this one-directional model, companies supplied the information they wanted consumers to hear and read. All content originated from the host company and not the customer. Now, with Web 2.0 interactive tools, the user (customer) and the originator (company) alike have the power to generate content.

Web 2.0 is truly customer-centric, user-interactive, and dynamic. It fosters community participation and builds on collective community intelligence. Social computing, interactivity, and customer participation are central to

Web 2.0. Other Web 2.0 tools include podcasts, vodcasts, social networks (LinkedIn, Facebook, MySpace), search engines (Google, Bing, Yahoo) and Voice Over Internet Protocol (VOIP) such as Skype.

Consistent with our description of the sources of the rifts, we saw a faster initial adoption of Web 2.0 tools by younger Internet users, but the demographic gap is closing, according a Pew tracking survey.[15] Reporting on that survey, Amanda Lenhart wrote, "The share of adult Internet users who have a profile on an online social network site has more than quadrupled in the past four years—from 8 percent in 2005 to 35 percent now."[16]

Web 2.0 tools are abundant and growing every day, as business people we can appropriately focus on a limited range of objectives in deciding the tools to use. Who are your customers? What types of relationships do they desire with you? What types of tools will best facilitate those interactions? These questions center on the customer not the technology, which is a basic premise of any good business model.

This sentiment is echoed by Charlene Li, a leading social media expert, who says: "Many companies approach social computing as a list of technologies to be deployed as needed—a blog here, a podcast there—to achieve a marketing goal. But a more coherent approach is to start with your target audience and determine what kind of relationship you want to build with them, based on what they are ready for."[17]

Some of the characteristics of Web 2.0 tools include:

- Always-on and on-demand

- Mobile

- Controlled by consumers and users

- Global in nature

- Oriented to generational differences

- Constantly changing and developing

We are in a post-Web 2.0 world. The shift has happened; it's just that not everyone knows it. The fundamental properties that link all of these different types of media is that the participants *choose* to engage and participate in the communication. For purposes of this book we will refer to these technologies, when applied to marketing, as **participant media**.

The term participant media recognizes the centrality of new media technologies in facilitating communication among individuals and organizations that builds and sustains interactive, self-selected, engaging communities.

The level of participation can be active such as writing or commenting on a blog, or more passive like browsing a blog. A participant may create a video for YouTube or just view one. He or she may be using Facebook to stay in touch or to start a movement. The participant can play different roles in the communication and be the creator or consumer of the message. Everyone is a participant, even the marketers, although they are no longer solely in control of the message. The digital nature of the communication that these technologies support is unrestricted in form and content, and in the freedom to choose to participate. It can be directed to the next bed in a dorm room or across the world. It can disseminate news or opinions, foster collaboration, learn, teach, coach, mentor, promote products, build brands, connect to customers, defend, or attack. This democratization of knowledge and information combined with universal access is changing everything, especially marketing. It blows up organizational structures and traditional views of time and space, privacy and intimacy.

How does this new media shift affect you and your organization's goals?

- Marketing in most economies encompasses more than products or brands. It embraces feelings and brand experiences. In most cases, customers today co-create this experience and add their own importance and meaning to it, irrespective of the values that the marketer attempts to convey.

- Marketing and most business focuses on an emotional connection that springs from the customer's experiences with the product or service.

- The growth in social media results not only from a few technology-savvy market mavens or fickle teenagers. An increasing number of users are older adults with significant and disposable monetary resources. They use these media frequently and for a variety of reasons. Examples include Eons.com, which bills itself as the "online community for Boomers," and eHarmony.com, one of the largest Internet-based communities for people seeking love and companionship.

- Emerging media is neither a fad nor just a tool to create buzz among customers. It has strategic and tactical significance and when used effectively has the ability to build long-term relationships with customers, employees, suppliers, and other important stakeholders.

- These technologies will flatten organizational hierarchies and enable people to work together globally in real time. Time and place are no longer as relevant as they used to be.

We believe participant media technologies have untapped applications in marketing, business development, business maintenance, and growth. They are particularly suitable for connecting with technology-savvy customers, suppliers and stakeholders. Companies and organizations that ignore the power of these new technologies do so at their own peril. And there is more to come.

The world of participant media is ever evolving. It will require you to be diligent to stay on board and surf the rift. Here is what your company can do to harness the power of participant media.

Action items

1. Talk to one customer every day for the next two weeks and ask each one how he or she uses social media for business purposes.

2. Find a blog relevant to your industry or a product category and visit it every day for a week, commenting whenever you can on specific posts.

3. Search Google for your company name, brand names, product categories and industry categories. Find results for your company, products and services. We'll give you some advice for improving your search results in a later chapter.

4. Go to YouTube and search for videos about your competitors and your market segments. You may be surprised to see how successfully your competitors are using Internet video as part of their integrated marketing communications strategies.

Ten questions

Here are ten key questions to ask yourself to assess whether you are effectively participating in the mediascape.

1. Do you have a personal Facebook page or LinkedIn profile? If so, do you use it purely for personal reasons, or for business networking?

2. Which social network makes the most sense for your company and your business model? Why?

3. Which participant media applications offer your company the most value? Collaboration? Research? Brand awareness? Customer support?

4. How is your company using participant media applications?

5. How does it fit strategically with the rest of your marketing plan?

6. Who are the internal champions for your Internet marketing programs?

7. What is your budget?

8. What are the barriers to your success?

9. How will you know if you are successful? What metrics are you tracking?

10. Does your corporate culture fit with your Internet marketing strategy?

Chapter 2

Anyone can publish: That means you!

"Conventional advertising is focused on saying 'my brand is good.' When someone on the Internet says it—an independent voice—it's different in terms of the credibility and influence it has." Phileppe Lamy, vice president, L'Oreal China.[18]

What or who on the Internet is powerful enough to attract the attention of companies? Enter the blog! A popular weapon in the participant media arsenal of an empowered citizenry that is being used so effectively companies all over the world are sitting up and taking notice. Perhaps more important, savvy companies are studying blogs to learn what people are saying—or not saying—about them and why.

If you have ever wondered about how people like yourself find time to read blogs on a regular basis let alone write one, you are not alone. But before you push aside blogging as a farfetched idea meant for the "tech types with nothing better to do with their time" consider this: Mark Cuban, the owner of Dallas Mavericks, a multibillionaire who has many other commitments besides owning the Mavericks, routinely blogs on blogmaverick.com and considers blogging an important activity for his brand and his business empire.[19] Technorati, a leading name in blog ratings, considers Cuban's to be among the top 1000 Web blogs in the word.[20]

Blogs

While most of you have undoubtedly heard of the terms blog and blogging, you may wish to know what blogging entails and how it works. The *Oxford Dictionary* added the words Web log, Web logging and Web logger to the dictionary in 2003,

Today "blog" has morphed into a legitimate word defined as a Web site on which an individual or group of users produces an ongoing narrative. Some refer to blogs as a "collective conversation."[21] A blog goes beyond message boards or Internet postings by enabling bloggers to post comments and link to other blogs. Most blogs feature the opinions of individuals and business, political, or other topical thought leaders.

Despite the wide variety, blogs have some common elements. These include reader comments, categories, trackback links to other sites that also discuss the entry, and permalinks (permanent URLs) to individual posts. For example, a blogger will use a permalink to refer to an article. These elements provide continuity and facilitate the on-going collective conversation. The importance of blogs continues increasing as bloggers achieve more influence than paid messages or company-sponsored messages within traditional media settings. In addition, blogs are incorporating video and audio to make them even more engaging.

Blogs gained an early footing in the business realm when technology-based companies used them as Web-based, project management tools. Since then blogging has continued to encompass many different fields and topical areas. It has evolved and has gained considerable popularity worldwide. Influential blogs address such diverse subjects as politics, cultural nuances, technology trends, and cat watching.

Why you should care about blogs

You may think that blogs are only popular among a certain group of people that find them entertaining. But does that make them useful? And how does this translate into a meaningful, valuable business model for you or your company? We know that how organizations and individuals access, collect, analyze, and disseminate information has changed dramatically over the years. Recent advances in technology place the customer in a central role. Technology now contributes to brand building by creating and sustaining a long-term relationship with the customer who actively participates in the process.

Ample evidence suggests that marketing has evolved from a company-centered "let me tell you why you should buy this product or service" approach to one where the customer decides how, when and where to seek information on your products and services and when, where, or how to engage in any transaction with you. This creates a challenge for marketers who must adjust their strategies to incorporate a new "attraction marketing" paradigm in which the customer connects with the company or the brand on his/her terms and often co-creates the experience. The connection must create personal meaning for the customer, especially if the company wants to create a longer-term relationship with the customer.

Creating a loyal customer is not a new idea. But the tools to create long-term customer alliances are new. The focus of the alliance has changed, too, as customers are more empowered, more organized, and more demanding than ever before. Now, you have to give them a reason why they should align with you and not with your competitor. In fact, the proliferation of participant media tools has proven to be a double-edged sword for marketers. It has provided them the tools to better target their top prospects while at the same time empowering customers with tools that help them take control of how—and when—they connect with marketers. For example, customers can control and often completely skip advertising and other promotional tactics directed at them through traditional channels such as television. However, the same technology has also created opportunities for a different kind of communication between the marketer and the customer.

A rift has emerged between the potential of these relationship-building technologies and the efficacy of their use. Marketers clearly need a better strategy to reach these new, technology-savvy customers that are more demanding and more vocal than ever before. Ideally this new approach involves a customized communication that engages the customer, builds customer trust and loyalty, and leverages the Internet by optimizing its potential for community building among customers. We believe blogs fill an important role in community building with your customers. Done correctly, blogging can provide significant return on investment for your communication dollars.

Jonathan Schwartz of Sun Microsystems, in describing one of the biggest advantages of blogging, said "(it) lets you participate in communities you want to cultivate."[22] That premise and promise of blogging—the ability to cultivate relevant communities—has led individuals to embrace the blog as a place to express opinions and read the opinion of others, including those of marketers.

The impact of blogs on business and marketing

Firms that blog have found a new way to stay relevant to their customers. Despite General Motors' recent financial troubles, its blogs are good examples of how any company can effectively use blogs to connect or reconnect with stakeholders.[23]

Marketers may use blogs to address the challenges arising from the changing media dynamics. Garmin, the "market navigation" company, is a perfect example of blogging for differentiation. By featuring stories of users—including novice users, car racing fans, and aviation experts—Garmin's blogs inform its users far beyond typical marketing messages. For example, its blogs discuss everything from bike-racing tips for outdoor enthusiasts to NASCAR events. The product mention is within the context of the main story. By being relevant, interesting and current, the blog builds awareness and loyalty for the company among its customers and prospects.[24]

Blogs offer companies new ways to communicate with audiences that may not respond to traditional media. A recent study suggested that 71 percent of those aged 16-34 in the U.S. have participated in blogging, and they are three times more likely than people 35-49 years old to manage and write their own blog. These blogs can provide marketers an accurate look at the likes and dislikes of "Gen-Next" customers.[25] Perhaps even more importantly, while blogging among the younger group generally involves discussion of pop culture and personal information, older bloggers use the blogosphere to discuss, share and analyze everything from the current political climate to travel and dining experiences—solid information marketers can use to cultivate customers and convert them to start word-of-mouth buzz.

The Southwest Airlines blog attracts a wide range of readers, from college students to retired army officers. It provides an example of how a well-written and interesting blog can create passion about the brand irrespective of the audience age. Further, just as with other media, firms can segment their blogging audience by writing multiple blogs focusing upon specific target markets.[26]

Thought leaders use blogs to share their expertise and experiences. Many leading consultants, writers, political pundits, and academics share their expertise via blogs and provide readers with the most current information in their respective fields. Thought leaders such as Management Consultant Tom Peters,[27] Social Media Expert Charlene Li,[28] Silicon Valley Insider Guy Kawasaki,[29] and Marketing Guru Seth Godin[30] are some of the well-recognized names in the blogosphere. Internal thought leaders can discuss their views about relevant issues within the firm and provide opportunities for employee dialogue. This individualized communication from a person is perceived as more human than a faceless, remote, and impersonal company line from the corporate communication department.

Blogs are global by nature. Publishing a blog provides a platform for firms to reach out to global audiences. Japanese (37 percent) and English (36 percent) are currently the two predominant blog languages followed by Mandarin Chinese (8 percent).[31] The democratization and globalization of blogs is also evident in the fact that non-western languages have been quick to occupy the blogosphere; Farsi recently moved up to number ten bumping Dutch to number eleven.

Blogs enable marketers to see their organizations from the viewpoint of the customer. Firms that enable customers to communicate directly with them can get a deeper understanding of customer likes, dislikes, interests, and concerns. This provides marketers with an opportunity to address customer comments, while setting the expectation that the customer's input will strengthen the product, service, or brand in the long run.

Southwest Airlines, Dell Computer, and Comcast have used blogs or social networking sites to resolve customer complaints. Reportedly, not only did these companies address the complaints, they sometimes offered customers advice on how to save money or referred to a blog post about an issue, as in the case of Southwest Airlines.[32]

Strategic value of blogs

The good news is that just about anyone or any company can use blogs. There are informal and personal blogs, informational blogs, mobile blogs, and corporate blogs. Corporate blogs for example, are designed to add value to the communication chain both internally, and for public and customer communications. Corporate blogs offer a variety of uses from providing top-down (from the CEO) and bottom-up (from employees) communications to fostering communication between the marketer and the customer. They can gain marketing intelligence; provide an ongoing dialog with customers, vendors, employees and other stakeholders; or simply keep customers informed about issues that they care about.

Let's take a quick look at some common blog applications for companies.

The levels of usage and strategy behind corporate blogs are as varied as the firms themselves. While firms use blogs for internal communications and market research, business applications of blogs range from passive to tactical to strategic. Which use is the most relevant depends on your organization's context and marketing objectives.

Firms that simply monitor blogs for postings about their brands, products, or competitive products are "passive-use" companies. They recognize the value of word-of-mouth and customer feedback, and use this knowledge to stay relevant to the customer. These companies may utilize various sources, including blogs, replies to blog entries, customer review sites, and message boards to gain customer insight. For example, Playboy Entertainment Group gathers information from open forum groups about customer likes and dislikes. Dixie retail business sponsors a weekly Internet radio show called MommyCast.[33] The program's blog provides the company unfiltered feedback on its product lines, which in turn helps redefine product attributes. According to the director of marketing at a San Francisco consulting firm, this type of customer insight provides marketers with an opportunity to learn about their customers in real time.[34] While these companies and others like them do not have their own corporate blogs, they utilize blogs in conjunction with other resources to gain valuable customer insight.

Companies that use blogs as a marketing tool to specifically drive traffic to their site or as a promotional tactic are "tactical-use" companies. This category includes companies such as Budget Car Rental, Honda and Guinness. For example, the Budget blog enables users to post their stories of travels and adventures while also offering them the ability to register for gifts and other promotional offerings. This type of blog clearly uses the medium to integrate with specific promotional events.[35]

Most tactical-use companies have corporate-sponsored blogs, but unlike user-generated blogs, these are used to increase awareness of their brand and drive traffic for specific promotions. In another example from Budget, the rental car company launched a promotional blog called "Up Your Budget" that successfully drove traffic and created excitement around a promotional campaign. Vespa, the Italian moped manufacturer, is yet another company that uses blogs tactically. Vespa customers blog on the company site about their passion for the company and its products. They offer an insider look at the product while adding legitimacy to the brand. This helps other customers identify with Vespa and helps to spread news of new products. These companies expect to gain customer insight, build brand loyalty and generate buzz about their products, brands and promotional activities as customers share their opinions with other customers.[36]

"Strategic-use" companies use blogs as a true interactive medium, fully supported by senior management with a corporate commitment that reaches across functional areas. These companies use blogs for internal and external communication and feedback, to conduct market research, initiate customer communication, gather competitive intelligence, generate new product ideas, and supplement promotional efforts. The true value of blogging as a business tool is most evident in the strategic-use companies. Strategic-use companies recognize that insights gained through these tools provide valuable information on customers, markets, competition and trends. These companies value the ability of blogs to share information with the customer, garner feedback, address customer concerns, gain competitive intelligence, and drive product development. All these uses are geared toward building brand loyalty and customer connectedness

Boeing, Microsoft, Southwest Airlines and Garmin are some of the companies using blogs strategically. Ken Levy, of MashupX and former product manager for Visual Studio Tools Ecosystem (a Microsoft company), uses his blog to discuss the latest news, information and trends for developers that build add-ins for the firm's products. The blog provides links to relevant events and tools of interest to his community of users. Ken's Microsoft background is relevant only within the context of the discussion and does not overshadow the discussion of the product.[37] Other companies clearly have similar objectives as evidenced by the number of employees that blog on behalf of their employers and by the number of blogs that are read by the final customer. Some 2,000 employees of Sun Microsystems, including managers and developers, blog about everything from company culture to product news.

Twitter

Actor Aston Kutcher beat CNN and many others to become the first Twitter user to attract a million followers. And, another popular celebrity helped Twitter gain even more attention when Oprah Winfrey wrote her first "tweet" during her April 17, 2009 show.[38] It's a phenomenon we can't ignore.

Twitter, founded by Jack Dorsey, Biz Stone, and Evan Williams, and launched in July 2006, is a social networking and micro-blogging service that allows users to post their latest updates. An update—called a tweet—is limited to 140 characters and can be posted through three methods: Web form, text message, or instant message.

Twitter is changing the way we live, if you accept the premise of *Time* magazine's June 5, 2009 cover story. "Twitter . . . fundamentally changed the rules of engagement," wrote *Time* reporter Steven Johnson. "It added a second layer of discussion and brought a wider audience into what would have been a private exchange. And it gave the event an afterlife on the Web. Yes, it was built entirely out of 140-character messages, but the sum total of those tweets added up to something truly substantive, like a suspension bridge made of pebbles."[39]

Twitter may be the best way to generate "word of thumbs.*" It asks the question "what are you doing now?" and your 140-character answer is broadcast to any Twitter subscriber that chooses to be one of your "followers."

On the surface, it sounds like a nice little quirky tool, but it has developed into an instant communication vehicle to reach a constituency immediately. Major media outlets like CNN are using it to get news out fast.[40] News anchors like Rick Sanchez use Twitter to receive instant feedback and cover breaking news while on the air.[41] Marketers can use Twitter to communicate with customers and humanize management.

On Twitter, you can "follow" or be "followed by" other Twitter users. Twitter includes a search capability that lets you find other users with similar interests. You can then "follow" those users to monitor the subjects, trends and issues important to them.

To accumulate Twitter followers, you can heed the advice of Guy Kawasaki, Silicon Valley venture capitalist and prolific business author, who recently blogged on the subject, "Looking for Mr. Goodtweet: How to Pick Up Followers on Twitter."[42] His ten tips include following people who already have thousands of followers, linking your tweets to interesting content, establishing yourself as a subject-matter expert, incorporating multimedia links into your tweets, and choosing from among many available Twitter-related applications to help you automate the management of your Twitter account.

Companies like Dell are even beginning to generate revenue from Twitter.[43] It wasn't an overnight sensation; Dell's been on Twitter for two years.[44]

Forbes magazine recently reported that online retailer Zappos which was recently acquired by Amazon, uses Twitter to connect employees and customers in a friendly, personal way that has proved highly effective.[45] At twitter.zappos.com, the company aggregates employee "tweets" on a single stream under the heading "Powered by Twitter, Zappos.com, clothing and you." Zappos CEO Tony Hsieh sends "tweets," and he has thousands of followers on both Twitter and his blog. According to Jennifer Leggio of ZNET, Twitter is "becoming the new business card." Even NASA is using Twitter![46]

Companies should consider Twitter for engaging internal and external clients. Former General Electric Company CEO Jack Welch and his wife Suzy summed it up in their weekly *BusinessWeek* column. "Twitter, in essence, allows you to attend a great big cocktail party filled with diverse and (typically) civilized chatter. Some of what you hear and say will be frivolous. But the chatter will also provoke, inform, and engage you in a way, and at a volume you can't replicate offline . . . Best of all, for us, Twitter helps you test—and improve—your ideas."[47]

What does this mean to you?

Blogs and micro-blogs like Twitter provide companies and individuals an inexpensive way to publish ideas and information for their target audiences that can be internal (e.g., employees) or external (customers, vendors, investors, and regulators).

Corporate blogging is very easy—sometimes too easy. Someone needs to be responsible for assigning permission to post blog items, as well as monitoring the content and any two-way communication that the blog content generates. You also may consider "moderating" comments (in which case comments must be reviewed before they are made public), or in some cases disabling comments when they are deemed inappropriate or harmful to the blog audience and the spirit of open communication. While many blog items are time-sensitive and, therefore, ephemeral, other postings may have long-term value. It should be someone's responsibility within your organization to monitor your blog and delete items that no longer provide value.

There are several reasons you consider starting a blog.

Blogs are evolving constantly. The best blogs incorporate a variety of media, including audio, video and flash presentations. Subscribe to newsletters (MediaPost.com has a variety of free newsletters and alerts that provide valuable advice and examples of blogs and other Web 2.0 technologies) and review a variety of blogs in your industry and in other markets that you can follow for ideas.

Your blog will engage and satisfy the interests of your audience. For every post, you should be able to answer the question, "Why will anyone be interested in this item?" Put yourself in the reader's shoes. If your blog doesn't provide value and appeal to the customer's self interest, it will be ignored, regardless of any content you post that might seem useful in promoting your company, your brands, or your products

Blog to communicate your expertise. Blogs offer all the value of traditional thought leadership platforms such as speaking opportunities, bylined articles and media interviews; plus, they add the value of immediacy without having to contend with any third-party delays or filters.

Blog for a purpose. A well-focused blog develops a personality that will attract repeat visits from regular readers who expect to encounter a consistent "voice" from your blog, whether you have one person contributing content or many.

Action items

Here are some suggestions for you to follow if you believe that blogging may be a valuable option.

1. Review blogs and tweets that your company and colleagues currently publish. Do you believe these blogs are serving valuable purposes?

2. Go to Technorati.com, the leading blog search engine, and search for your company, brands, products, and thought leaders. How are other blogs covering you? What are people saying about you in their blog posts and comments?

3. Brainstorm some ideas for a new blog with your colleagues. Can you envision enough valuable, ongoing content to keep the blog fresh and interesting for an indefinite time period?

Ten questions

Now ask yourself the following questions

1. What blogs are your target audiences reading today?

2. Who in your company will be responsible for the blog?

3. Who will write blog posts?

4. How will you handle comments?

5. Who will Tweet?

6. What will you write about?

7. Are your competitors blogging or Tweeting? How effective are their blogs?

8. Will you assign someone to regularly monitor competitors' blogs?

9. Will you limit or control in any way the blogging activities of your employees?

10. What incentives will you offer key employees to be part of your blogging team?

Chapter 3

Your new media: Webcasts, podcasts and vodcasts

Are you a political junkie who wants the latest poll numbers on your favorite politician, or an economics aficionado who must keep up with what the pundits are saying about the economic trends of a country? Perhaps you are an energy company that wants to provide its investors information about a promising green technology that you are investing in. Today's political junkie, economics aficionado, or green investor will find the most recent and relevant information on podcasts and videos specifically produced to reach targeted segments. If your company currently does not have a podcast or a video presence on YouTube or other similar site to communicate key information to its audiences, you should seriously consider it and act quickly. As people become more mobile, they insist on getting the information they consider important at any time, on a device of their choosing, and in a manner that is most convenient to them. For those who are not visual and prefer auditory information, podcasting affords them the flexibility and the convenience they desire. No wonder *Forbes* magazine noted that the allure of a podcast is its ability to "time shift." In fact, podcasts and videocasts both have the ability to let users listen and view what they want, when they want, where they want, and how they want.

The advent of low-cost audio recording devices like micro recorders that record in MP3 format and low-cost video cameras like the Flip and Web cams make it easy for anyone to capture audio and video. Audacity, Garageband, iMovie and similar software make it easy to edit and produce a video. Finally, distribution channels such as iTunes and YouTube offer global distribution of your broadcast. You can even provide live, interactive Webcasts with technology like UStream.

What exactly are podcasts and vodcasts?

Podcasts, vlogs and vodcasts give users the ability and control to produce their own content. Control as we have said before is at the heart of participant media and its savvy buyers, browsers, investors, and stakeholders. How important is this? Well many, including Cisco CEO John Chambers, believe that the next phase of the Internet will be driven by visual communications.[48]

Let's start with some specifics on podcasts. Podcasts are digital recordings, typically in the form of an MP3 file, that are distributed via syndication (RSS) feeds or through podcast host sites (podcatchers) such as iTunes. Podcasts are not device specific—you don't need an Apple iPod to listen or view podcasts. Numerous devices play podcasts including mobile telephones, desktop and laptop computers, and MP3 players. In essence, podcasts are really audio blogs that can sometimes be accompanied by video and then they are called vlogs or vodcasts. Podcasts became prominent when Apple Computer started supporting podcasts with Version 4.9 of iTunes, released in June 2005. Podcasts are an ideal format for gaining knowledge about everything from how to prepare perfect Indian cuisine to what a thought leader is saying about major shifts in the global economy. You can multi-task and listen to a podcast while working at your computer (which is what we often do when preparing lectures) or while working out (which we don't do enough!).

What makes podcasting an attractive participant media tool is that it is a relatively inexpensive way to reach various niche markets globally; whether your firm is the size of Netflix or a small consulting firm such as Cullinane Media. Podcasts are a good example of what Chris Anderson called "the long tail" to describe a niche strategy in which a company sells a large number of unique items, but in small quantities to a wide reaching audience.[49] Podcasts let you sell your ideas to an audience that is far and wide. Listeners can also add comments to your podcast to provide feedback. Online research firm eMarketer expects that the podcasting audience will increase 251 percent to 65 million by 2012. And of those listeners, 25 million or more will be active users who tune in at least once a week. A study quoted by eMarkteter also found that about 54 percent of the podcasting audience is in the 35-54 age demographic. Not surprisingly, this group is affluent, educated, media and market savvy, and engaged in issues that matter to them.[50]

Did you say that 25 million does not look like a very big market? Well, if you consider that these are people that *choose* to listen to your ideas and provide a captive audience that actively processes your information, it is hard to ignore their power.

Who podcasts, who listens, and does it matter?

While many podcasters are individuals talking about their hobbies, more and more businesses and other types of podcasters are providing information on mainstream issues. Traditional broadcasters know the power of mobility, and they were among the first to embrace podcasting. National Public Radio (NPR) was an early adopter of podcasts. If you consider the profile of the NPR listener, it makes sense: 62 percent of its news audience has a college degree; 77 percent is employed; and 75 percent has an income above $50,000, with a large segment making more than $89,000.[51] Other news media including the BBC, *The Economist*, NBC, *The Wall Street Journal* and *BusinessWeek* have a number of podcasts on a variety of topics ranging from health and investment options to geopolitical changes governing environmental issues.

Overall, podcasting offers marketers a new way to reach potentially lucrative niche markets and customers. Your podcast audience comes to you actively seeking information. This high-level engagement with the host site—whether the user downloads the podcast or listens online—is the major difference between this and other media forms. Podcasts can be a rewarding way to engage your customers, shareholders and stakeholders, both internal and external.

Consider how some businesses are using podcasts to reach their audiences:

The Economist: Worried since the Dow Jones Industrial Average lost 22 percent of its value in eight days? Go to *The Economist* podcast[52] for a commentary and analysis on what went wrong and how to fix it. The publication's podcast has information on other world topics, too, just in case you want to know more about Iceland's economic meltdown. In fact, considered one of the most reliable sources of business and political news, *The Economist's* podcasts have consistently been ranked among the best in business by Digg.com. Who considers advertising on *The Economist's* Web site a good investment? The best of the best—Harvard Business School, University of Chicago Booth Graduate School of Business, Credit Suisse, BASF, Tata Consultancy, Accenture and many more. While it is unlikely that anyone will decide to enroll in the Harvard Business School's executive MBA program because of a podcast, the association will not go unnoticed. These high credibility institutions help each other build brand value.

MommyCast: Named best podcast of 2007 by Apple iTunes, this Webby award winner is one of the most successful programs "for and by women immersed in the fullness of motherhood and life."[53]

Whirlpool: An iconic American brand, Whirlpool engages people in a virtual community through its "American Family" podcast.[54] Topics on the podcast are as interesting and diverse as the people that use Whirlpool products—from engaging kids in elections to a how-to guide for surviving a layoff. Why does Whirlpool sponsor this? The American Family Web site provides links to Whirlpool Cares, a site where the company provides goodwill-generating information on how it cares for the community, the environment, and the family.

General Electric: Another company that uses podcasts well to convey its brand image to its audience is GE.[55] Using a tag line "Imagination at Work," it provides examples of how GE tackles issues related to environmental degradation, energy security and human development. The information showcases GE investments in various countries and projects. The content provides objective, quality information about issues, along with information about the company.

Not-for-profits: Governmental and not-for-profit organizations are often early adopters of online new media, including podcasts. The United Nations,[56] World Health Organization,[57] Humane Society,[58] International Olympic Committee,[59] and many more have eagerly embraced the idea of audio and video information delivery. Their podcasts are sophisticated, well developed, informative, and a model from which the business world can learn.

Don't think that because you have a small business, these media are beyond your scope. Podcasting is one of the easiest tools to use for businesses of all sizes. The *Cullinane and Green Report*, which analyzed technology and business development issues, is a good example of podcasting by a small consulting firm. Within a matter of months after posting online, the report reached a global listening audience of thousands. Although not active for two years, the *Cullinane and Green Report*[60] is still being downloaded by people in countries around the world!

Video, vlogs and vodcasts

The 2008 U.S. presidential campaign saw every major candidate deploying very effective uses of online video, podcasts, and viral e-mail. Clearly, participant media tools now impact almost every facet of our lives. Tools that didn't exist ten years ago have profoundly changed aspects of our personal and professional lives, from how we communicate to how we interact with others. One such tool is online video. Online video sharing sites like YouTube and Viddler are changing the way organizations connect, not merely with their employees but with their customers, vendors, and other stakeholders. Internet video is becoming a popular way to remain connected with your target market. Companies large and small, for profit and not for profit must assess the possibilities that online video offers them.

The official U.S. White House Web site (www.whitehouse.gov) looks nothing like something from a bureaucratic government.[61] For starters, the *Briefing Room* highlights a blog with updates every few hours. Visitors can view a video the President's weekly address, request updates by signing up for an e-mail alert, and send comments to the "Contact Us" section. It is a crisp, well-developed, and interactive site that gives the visitor a sense of familiarity and engagement with the U.S. executive branch. So, it is not surprising that some have called U.S. President Barack Obama's presidency the YouTube presidency.

The growth in Internet video has been nothing short of explosive. According to eMarketer, almost 168 million people in the U.S., more than 84 percent of Internet users, are expected to watch an online video at least once a month in 2009. This number is expected to rise to 190 million by 2012.[62] Interestingly enough, the majority of these users are viewing advertising videos in addition to other content. The interest and indeed fascination with online video content seems appropriate for this new generation of consumers that embrace this content as relevant, timely and readily accessible.

Within the broader context, video is part of the new Webcast model of information dissemination and sharing among consumers. Online content, whether audio or a video, is often more effective and less expensive to produce than traditional television or radio content. More important, this content can reach a larger segment of stakeholders. The viral, peer-to-peer transmission of online videos demonstrates how people pay more attention to content they receive from trusted sources. Interesting, intriguing, funny, or just plain absurd videos get passed around by e-mail and talked about among a populace that can access this content on their mobile and computer devices.

Who is watching your video?

"As markets morph into Web 2.0 'conversations' and consumers gain much greater freedom to pursue their own interests, customers are doing things that online marketing managers don't necessarily want or expect them to do," writes Donna Hoffman in the July 2009 *McKinsey Quarterly*. For example, they can easily connect with one another, often using multimedia sites such as YouTube or Flickr, so they themselves can satisfy their need for information about products. What's more, consumers may trust information obtained in this way much more than they do information from your company. What will happen when these consumer experiences are much more interesting than anything your marketers have put up on the Web?"[63]

Interesting research from Accenture shows rapid adoption of online video and other Web 2.0 technologies and applications among middle-aged Americans. The research discovered Baby Boomers increasing their adoption of popular consumer technology applications at an average of 50 percent, nearly 20 times faster than Generation Y. Accenture findings suggest that Boomers are becoming more technology savvy and using technology more effectively. For example, Boomers increased watching and posting videos on the Internet by 35 percent, while Gen Y usage decreased slightly (2 percent). In addition, Boomers increased listening to music on an iPod or other portable music player by 49 percent, more than four times faster than Gen Y (12 percent). These data suggest that the generation gap in technology usage may be narrowing and providing marketers an opportunity to connect with consumers in multiple demographic and psychographic segments.[64]

Not surprisingly, expectations for the growth of online video remain strong. eMarketer predicts that growing numbers of both traditional and alternative media companies will use professional video to reach their online markets.[65] While YouTube, launched in 2005 and purchased by Google in 2006, is perhaps the most well-known video sharing site, there are several others that are used for a host of purposes. Viddler, the video editing and sharing device, offers features such as commenting and tagging specific moments in a video. Used extensively by members of social networks, it is finding business uses in the connected communities. Similar to YouTube, Viddler categorizes videos as featured, most popular, most discussed, recently uploaded, etc., to help encourage interaction with viewers.[66]

Following are two good examples of how corporations and non-profits are deploying online video solutions to reach internal and external audiences.

Cisco's John Chambers was an early adopter of video blogging to communicate with employees. The company's blog commented on Chambers' initial video in June 2007: "In a video message to employees today, Cisco Chairman and CEO John Chambers challenged all Cisco employees to 'cancel one trip this quarter and use Web 2.0 collaboration technologies to conduct your business in lieu of traveling.' Chambers made the video from his laptop computer and, as most of us mere mortals do, one never quite knows where to look when using a Webcam."[67]

Many nonprofit organizations have been leading adopters of Web 2.0 techniques to engage constituents and donors. The Humane Society of the United States is using a combination of tools on its Web site to change the world.[68] It effectively uses videos, podcasts and blogs to vividly demonstrate efforts to end animal cruelty and to give people a variety of opportunities to act in support of a wide range of HSUS initiatives. Videos on its "Animal Channel" include calls to action that enable supporters to get immediately involved. The main video page also links to a video blog that the society produces, providing an instant subscription sign-up link. The HSUS home page also links to a blog by the society's president, Wayne Pacelle, where open comments are encouraged and a lively conversation emerges from each new blog post.[69] You also may subscribe to RSS feeds for the society's video podcasts and blogs.

There are many ways vodcasts and podcasts can benefit your organization,

- Messaging and brand development

  Podcasts and video are excellent tools for building brand awareness in the marketplace and for addressing issues central to your stakeholders. Whether you are providing updates on important company initiatives or routine weekly updates to employees, online tools are engaging, easy to implement, and effective.

- Conducting public and investor relations

  Has your industry recently been in the news? Post a link to podcasts and videos to leverage news coverage while adding your own messages to communicate directly with your audience. The ability to manage your message in a medium that your audience finds compelling can be very powerful.

- Introducing new products

  The popular YouTube video titled "Will it Blend?" demonstrates how an ordinary product—an electric food blender—can create enough buzz to attract millions of viewers around the world.[70] BlendTech created the video to document the power of its industrial and commercial blenders. It used the company CEO as a spokesperson to blend a funny and unlikely variety of products, even an iPhone. The videos have been shared by millions of viewers around the world, and "Will it Blend?" has become a catch phrase among followers. Loyal fans now eagerly await viewing each new "Will it Blend?" segment and then pass it along to others, proving the viral power of Internet video to engage the audience.

- Showcasing expertise

  Podcasts and video are excellent ways to demonstrate company or individual expertise. Some small companies use podcasting extensively to provide a platform for frequently updating and customizing content to various market segments. In fact, podcasts have the ability to provide relevant information to target audiences. This is especially true if traditional media usage is declining among your target audience. Scheduling podcast and video guest "appearances" by your subject matter experts on popular blogs is a good way to showcase expertise and promote products.

- Reaching targeted niche markets

  Specialized audiences demand specialized content. Podcasts and video can easily become the one-stop shop if combined with blogs and other tools. WebMD.com, a top-rated Web site, features a daily a selection of videos that provide a wide range of information on health and lifestyle concerns.[71]

- Providing content on demand

  The potential to offer on-demand content is an advantage that really sets videos and podcasts apart from traditional media. Traditional media companies have realized that to survive in a world where on-demand is the norm, they must embrace podcasts and video. *The Wall Street Journal,* CNN, *The New York Times,* and most daily metropolitan papers now combine print content with a Web site format for on-demand delivery 24/7. For example, paid subscribers to *The Wall Street Journal* have on-demand access to a whole host of online content. They can listen to podcasts or watch videos on everything from the financial outlook for the automotive sector to the latest news from Iran. Indeed, the on-demand nature of audience interest has created entire online businesses. The popularity of hulu.com, the company offering everything from your popular TV programs to full length movies, is a prime example of a searchable Web site that offers on-demand and mobile content.

- Creating feedback loops

  Lastly, this new Web cast model delivers something traditional channels do not—the ability to create an instant feedback loop for content. Viddler lets you tag a video at specific moments, and podcasts allow the audience to comment and ask questions; capabilities that morph these media into marketing research tools offering a glimpse into the minds of your target audience. Understanding how your customers react to content is key to understanding their motivations and interests.

It's important to keep in mind the limitations of online videos and podcasts:

- Variable quality

  The ability to Webcast does not automatically translate to good quality. Companies that commit to producing podcasts and online video also need a commitment to high-quality content and delivery. They need to protect their brand equity from the negative consequences of poor content, inadequate quality or technical implementation. If the information is not relevant, interesting, or engaging, it will not deliver effectively. Technologies have certainly democratized content, but the content must enhance the brand. Although Webcasts should avoid being be too slick or overproduced. Part of the charm of user-generated audio and video is the amateur and accessible feel. Some of the best online videos are brief and homespun testimonials from customers, donors and event participants. Engage your customers by letting people they relate to do the talking (and selling!).

- Measurability

  Like most online media, Webcasts suffer from the same limitations in terms of measurability. Web tools that measure click throughs, downloads, and unique visitors can only provide some data. Who listens to or watches your content may be relatively easy to measure if you have some form of registration requirement. However, what often makes Webcasting a powerful tool also limits its measurability. Viral distribution of videos and podcasts increase the difficulty of measuring whether those who downloaded a podcast listened to it or whether a downloaded video was actually viewed.

  The ability to time shift content has enabled the migration of content to an on-demand platform defined by mobility. In other words, you can take it with you wherever you go and listen whenever you would like. The growth of podcasts and Web videos is likely to continue as people become more media savvy and less patient with canned deliveries through traditional devices. Cyberspace has no geographic boundaries and content can move around the world at the mere click of a mouse. Integrated seamlessly with other tools, Webcast devices satisfy a variety of purposes from knowledge creation and dissemination to brand building. The question, of course, is how can these media advance your overall business strategy? Here are Action items for you to consider.

Action items

1. Search YouTube for videos about your industry segment, competitors, products, and company.

2. Search iTunes for relevant podcasts

3. Ask your five most important customers how and if they are using Internet video, and what value they are getting from it.

Ten questions

Now ask yourself the following questions.

1. Is video and or audio right for your company? Why?

2. What do you have to say?

3. Who will be responsible for creating and overseeing content?

4. How much will you need to budget for video production?

5. What would the message be?

6. Who is your best target audience for video and or audio? Customers? Prospects? Employees? Shareholders?

7. What's the best place to reach your audience?

8. Can you commit to a regular podcast and/or video production schedule? Once a month? Once a week? Daily?

9. How will you provide for feedback?

10. Do you expect your audio and video messages to create dialogue between your company and your constituents?

Chapter 4

Capturing prospects: Search engine marketing

The "Do You Yahoo?" advertising campaign was designed to get people to use Yahoo! as their default search engine. And, to the chagrin of grammar teachers, the word "yahoo" was destined to become a noun and a verb, along with "google" or "googled," derived from the powerhouse search engine, Google. Online search engines have largely surpassed other reference sources as online users look on search engines to find people, places and things. Not only do your prospects and customers have access to such comprehensive search engines as Google, Yahoo!, MSN.com, Ask.com, Lycos and Microsoft's new entry, Bing.com, but they also can access specialized search engines such as Search Medica.com, which offers credible and objective medical information, and allows users to view results within general medicine or any of nine specific disease categories. What makes SearchMedica.com unique and engaging is that it breaks though a vast amount of generic or irrelevant content, addressing the primary problem most medical professionals encounter when using Google or other mainstream search engines. Are you a fan of international sports? Try www.AardvarkSport.net which prides itself on "sniffing out sports sites from around the world," and claims to have indexed more than 20,000 of the very best. These are just two examples of the thousands of content-specific and media-specific engines available today.

Why should your organization or company care about search engines? Well, try this exercise. Type your organization's name in the following query within Google's search box: *site:yourcompanyname.com*. How many pages are indexed with your organization's site name? Now type *site:dell.com* and watch as more than six million pages come up for one of the most optimized sites in the business world. What does this mean for you and your company? Simply that unless users can find you online, chances are they won't look for you offline either—especially if you are a small or mid-sized company that doesn't have a well-known brand and specializes in niche products, and services. If you are not searchable, you don't exist!

Now, consider this. The last time you wanted to find information about something or someone, how did you start? Chances are you went to Google, Yahoo! or Bing. Our point is that you probably did not search the traditional yellow or white pages (unless they happened to be the online versions). And that is the major point we are attempting to make: even if you have a magnificent Web site with great design and content, great functionality and aesthetics, it's not effective if it doesn't display among the top search listings. What matters is visibility and prominence. And that is what search engine marketing (SEM) and search engine optimization (SEO) are all about.

How search impacts your business

Search engine marketing and optimization are absolutely key to getting high visibility and to directing customers to the most local resources you offer (e.g. Find a store near you). A research study by SEMPO found that 73 percent of consumers used search engines to find a local business, and 78 percent researched a product online before making an in-store purchase. More importantly, 72 percent of these customers would prefer to buy in a store within a 20-minute drive even when they are doing their search online.[72] In essence, if they can't find a local outlet easily online, they won't buy from you no matter how well represented you are in the off-line world! Search matters for everyone trying to reach a market: Large and small; B-to-B and B-to-C; global and local; for-profit and not-for-profit. As a result, firms and organizations continue to invest more resources in search. According to SEMPO, search engine marketing is more than a $10 billion industry and likely to grow to $18 billion by 2011.[73] While these numbers vary somewhat depending upon the source, there is ample evidence to suggest that search has become an integral part of a well-developed and well-executed marketing strategy.

The power of Google is evident in its 60 percent market share, and Yahoo! has a respectable but distant second place with 20 percent share.[74] However, as you have probably seen in your own search efforts, generic search engines are relatively inefficient if what you are looking for is specialized information on products and services. So, it is hardly surprising that specialized search engines and databases such as SearchMedica and EDGAR are growing in popularity and quality. In fact, user demand and increasing ease of creation are contributing to the growing number of specialty search engines on the market today. Custom search engines can now be built with free tools that require no coding. Google, for example, offers Google Custom Search, one of the most popular options currently available.[75] There are now so many specialized search engines that it is hard to keep up with the best and brightest stars out there. Charles Knight, the editor of AltSearchEngines.com, an online blog and news site dedicated to alternative search engines, had to get creative when the number of alternative search engines became too many to be included in his Top 100 list.[76]

This ability to customize search for specific media categories, products or segments has extended to video as well. Why would users limit their searches for video to YouTube, when Blinkx.com can connect them with the best videos from around the word, including footage from leading news organizations and amateur videographers alike? Pixsy.com offers a searchable index of millions of videos and images. Kartoo.com and Clusty.com search the entire Web, and present search results in categories or clusters. The fact that search engines are getting ever more sophisticated is making mainstream search engines pay attention. They, too, recognize the importance of providing specific search results. At Google alone, users can focus their search on all of the Web or a number of specific media categories, including images, video, maps, news, shopping, blogs and more.

Customize, connect and optimize

Search technology has the ability to go beyond search to connect marketers and buyers through other applications, including shopping comparison sites, social networking platforms, site applications and more. Start by looking at shopping comparison engines such as Shopzilla[77], DealTime[78] and PriceScan[79]. These sites provide aggregate data on sellers of products and present these data to users looking to find a good deal. They compare prices across numerous retailers or identify a highly rated vendor from which to purchase a particular product. As customers get increasingly familiar with search, marketers recognize the value of being listed in comparison shopping engines. In fact, it is so critical for marketers to penetrate online shopping engines that they are constructing automated data feeds to streamline the otherwise arduous process of submitting data to shopping comparison engines. Marketers, particularly catalogers and other retailers with a high SKU count, typically package and distribute data feeds to top shopping comparison engines. Vendors offer marketers the ability to manage just a single feed while communicating valuable inventory and pricing information to 30 or more shopping comparison partners.

Marketers have come to realize that their customers appreciate and rely on search functionality, and nearly every online retailer offers users an option to search their site. Search enables users to quickly locate what they seek on a site, even if they had trouble navigating prior to conducting the search.

Clearly, search technology streamlines the process of locating information, products, and services in a host of different situations. Paid search can be a solid return on investment, because marketers only have to pay the search engines for sponsored listings. Even with these advertisements, you only pay for each time a user clicks on the ad. So if a men's apparel retailer wants to sell khaki pants online but wants to save the cost of reaching those interested in women's khaki pants, that retailer can bid on ad placement for its men's khaki pants, and their advertisement will come up only on searches for that particular term or keyword. Search has effectively removed the guesswork in targeting since users specify their interests each time they enter a search query, and smart marketers have secured the keywords and variations (e.g. men's khaki pants, men's casual pants) that will lead searching prospects to their site. Bidding for top placement of paid search ads can become quite competitive and vary in real time.

Facebook, MySpace, LinkedIn and many other social networking sites, while not specifically built around search technology, depend on search to allow users to find and connect with others on the sites. Without their integrated search functionality, making connections within these networking and social communities would be time consuming and cumbersome, and these sites would likely fail. In fact, search technology has already become so engrained as part of participant media that most users would be lost without it.

Better marketing through search

Aside from search extensions such as product data feeds, portals, or vertical search engines that cater to a particular type of professional or hobbyist, firms have two primary ways to market through the engines: Purchasing paid advertisements or sponsored links on the search engines, or improving their sites performance in the natural or organic listings of search engines through strategic content editing.

Web developers work daily to enhance their Web site content so it will perform better, and therefore place higher, in the natural or organic listings of search engines, often referred to as search engine optimization (SEO) or natural search optimization (NSO). In paid search, marketers bid on and secure keywords related to their site's content, and place related advertisements so they will appear in top positions clearly marked as sponsored listings. For example, on Google, these advertisements typically appear at the top the page and down the right column.

Paid search is billed to advertisers on a cost-per-click (CPC) basis. So, each time an advertiser's ad is clicked, that advertiser pays the previously established bid price for the particular keyword that triggered the ad. The position of any given ad on the Google page is determined primarily by three factors: the advertiser's bid, competitive bids and Google's proprietary quality score. Google and other leading engines review pay-per-click (PPC) search ads from an editorial perspective after advertisers create the ad copy and design.

Paid inclusion, a variation of the typical paid search format and currently offered only through Yahoo!, gives you a chance to pay for ads that are presented within a search engine's natural listings and not clearly identified as sponsored or paid advertisements. Again, with paid inclusion, relevance influences page placement. Marketers often use paid inclusion to ensure that important pages show up in search results that would otherwise be overlooked by the search engines as they index content for inclusion in natural results. These often include dynamic catalog pages, inventory that changes frequently and content that is invisible to the engines.

Natural search, also known as free, organic or algorithmic search, offers an effective complement or alternative to paid search. Natural search results appear on the left side of search engine results pages and occupy the majority of the page. These listings carry no media cost, but marketers have no guarantee of page placement. Plus, although they are commonly referred to as free, organizations make significant investments in staff and technology to rank high enough to attain these listings.

Want customers? Use search to self target

When you choose to incorporate search into your communications mix, it can significantly boost results and improve cost effectiveness thanks to the self targeting nature of search. At a basic level, it is a matter of defining and positioning the right keywords for a campaign and setting them up to be successful with effective Web site copy, landing pages, and bids.

So is it just that simple? Secure the right keywords on the top-performing consumer search engines and sit back to watch the dollars roll in? Not quite. Most marketers understand the power, importance and potential of search engines. Many have made conscious decisions to not only get started with search but to own their piece of search and whatever new participant media comes next. The growing universe of performance-based media, which includes search and affiliate marketing, is a new frontier. So although search provides a key tool for marketers today, the performance-based skill sets of search professionals also translate well into other marketing disciplines. Increasingly, marketers extend the dividends of a successful search effort by tapping their group's performance marketing talents to design and execute complementary performance-based media channels. It can take a team of experts to deliver and maintain a truly dominant paid and organic search campaign. Not only do the intricacies of consumer search engines require regular attention and optimization; many firms will expand beyond these engines, particularly marketers going after specialists or any kind of a niche audience. To some extent, through self targeting, consumer search engines enable marketers to focus on niche audiences based on keyword selection alone, but there's no substitute for a specialized portal that caters to a specific group of professionals.

Making search work for you

If you agree that search is critical to the success of your company or organization, the obvious question is how can you make it work for your business goals? While a complete discussion of the technicalities is beyond the scope of this book, it is important to understand how search engines work. In simple terms, search engines send out virtual spiders to crawl the Web, indexing Web pages along the way and reading the pages they find. These search engines employ complex and confidential algorithms to assess the relevance and importance of Web sites and ultimately determine page rank. In essence, companies need to make sure that the spiders can find their sites. Some things to keep in mind to ensure that your site can be found include:

- relevant and unique page content

- recognizable language such as HTML (instead of graphics, images or multimedia, which the spiders cannot recognize or index)

- number of inbound links

- age of the site

- size of the site

- site's reputation

It can be a daunting task to assess where to begin. Search engine marketing can be complex. The majority of the nation's biggest brands outsource the bulk of their search engine marketing programs to the search marketing experts. The majority of search marketers represent small businesses; many search marketers may not have the budget required to outsource a program. The good news is that even the smallest businesses can achieve very targeted and profitable results from a search campaign.

Budget, of course, can make the decision quick and easy. Large organizations with significant search budgets can choose between the costs associated with building a sufficient internal team versus partnering with an SEM firm. A year-long campaign with most SEM vendors can be purchased for anywhere from $20,000 to $60,000.[80] Many big brand search programs can exceed this budget by a great deal, with monthly search budgets easily reaching $100,000 in many cases. An internal professional can cost upwards of $85,000 a year. For some marketers, a hybrid approach works best. Some will partner with a consultant or search engine marketing agency to develop a strategy and plan of action and then manage that plan with internal resources. Others devise methods to share the workload across a mixed internal and outsourced team.

While there is no single formula that suits all, it is important to recognize that companies of all kinds can tap into search irrespective of the size of their budget or their operations. The smallest of businesses can secure niche, low-traffic keywords, which are purchased from a variety of online vendors. Many of the nation's leading brands, on the other hand, coordinate large national branding and customer acquisition campaigns with search while managing complementary regional campaigns for their local dealers or retail outlets. They may also enter into co-branding campaigns with complimentary products and services that direct users from one site to another.

What makes search particularly exciting is that it provides an unmatched level of accountability that you can leverage to gauge effectiveness each step of the way and to fine tune campaigns to optimize your efforts. This works for all types of search investments, whether paid, natural or otherwise, and the model for determining return on investment (ROI) depends more heavily on the goals of the campaign than on the type of search program being managed. Companies have different objectives for their investments in the many promotional methods available. From brand building to lead generation to customer acquisition, marketers have predetermined goals for different campaigns. Relative to other methods, resources spent on search are more measurable, and the accountability of search dollars is generally higher. If, for example, you have an e-commerce campaign where the primary aim is to sell products, then the equation of search engine effectiveness is quite simple. Firms managing these types of campaigns will typically determine an acceptable ROI level, and as long as they continue to achieve the desired returns on investment, they will continue to spend on search indefinitely. Many marketers measure ROI in this scenario by focusing on costs vs. sales. In general, several methods exist to measure search effectiveness, varying from the simplest to the most sophisticated models. Most firms employ multiple methods to measure search success; this likely illustrates the different goals of various search campaigns under a single marketer's management, the desire to get multiple readings on how a single focused search campaign performs or both. Some of these methods, though, warrant a closer look.

Partnering for better search performance

Pottery Barn, the well known retailer and cataloger, wanted to improve the performance of Potterybarn.com, PBTeens.com, and PotteryBarnKids.com, so they hired a leading SEO consulting firm to help. Its search engine optimization program, as reported by *Catalog Success* magazine in June 2007, indicated that Pottery Barn was able to realize the following results quite quickly:

- At PotteryBarn.com, the number of indexed pages (those pages where content is visible to the engines) rose by 1,268 percent, surpassing its six-month goal in one week and its ultimate target in less than two months.

- Indexed pages at PotteryBarnKids.com rose by 9,756 percent, more than doubling its overall target in less than a month.

- PBTeen.com's indexed pages grew by 4,319 percent, also surpassing its target in less than a month.

- Total traffic from natural search surged in the first three months.

- Total revenue from natural search also grew at a rate described by the two companies as "comparable to traffic for most properties."[81]

In May 2009, Wolfram Research launched an exciting new online search platform called Wolfram Alpha. Described as a "computational knowledge engine," its goal is nothing short of making "all systematic knowledge immediately computable and accessible to everyone." We suggest you visit www.wolframalpha.com and begin to familiarize yourself with this new search technology.[82]

In summary, some things to keep in mind about search marketing:

- Search is a growing and critical component of marketing. With about $18 billion in revenue projected by 2012, it is likely to grow bigger in terms of its relevance. So, if you are not searchable, you may become extinct.

- Firms expect to increase their spending on search engine marketing: 65 percent of companies reported they expect to spend more on search. Some of these companies are your competitors!

- Search is the major way customers look for information. The majority of the online population (85 percent) uses search to find everything from products to services to people. SEM also influences 20-30 percent of purchases made at retail locations. In other words, search matters.

- Search is not just about sales. Search also enhances brand awareness. According to SEMPO, 57 percent of all online marketers use search to enhance brand awareness.[83]

- Growth in specialty search. Businesses are taking advantage of the power of search and users are getting savvy with search. Specialty search offers great opportunities particularly if what you sell is not mainstream or serves a niche product or service market

- Search doesn't have to be expensive. What you need is targeting, and the self-targeting nature of search provides better ROI than most other online tools.

- Your search spend is measurable. Your search spend can be evaluated for each campaign. There are a diverse set of measurement tools that help you better understand and allocate resources to your search campaigns.

- Search can be used for a multitude of objectives. Search can be used for everything from brand awareness to an e-commerce campaign. When used with other integrated marketing communication tactics, it is an extremely effective and efficient tool.

- If you don't have internal expertise, consider partnering or using a consultant. It can be a one-time partnership or an entirely outsourced campaign.

- Search is critical for business and any organization that needs to engage others. In fact, if you are a small or mid-sized company, it matters even more for you.

Action items

Here are action items for you to consider.

1. Find out how many pages of your Web site are indexed on Google, Yahoo! and other search engines by typing your domain name in the search box as follows: *site:yourdomainname.com.*

2. Create a list of 100 keywords that your customers and prospects might use in searching for your company, products, and product categories.

3. Check out some of the vertical search engines, such as Kayak.com to see if such engines in your marketplace can add value to your search program. If you're an industrial manufacturer or other B-to-B company, try GlobalSpec.com, Business.com, or Hoovers.com.

4. Try the site-search feature on your own Web site (if the site uses one). Compare it to the site-search capabilities of competitive Web sites.

Ten questions

Now ask yourself the following:

1. Is your company currently doing Web search optimization and marketing?

2. How much do you expect to spend next year on SEO?

3. How do you measure the effectiveness of the money you're spending on paid search?

4. What are you doing to search-optimize your site?

5. Who is responsible for search engine strategies and tactics in your organization?

6. Do you need external consulting help?

7. What is your search rank? What about your competitors?

8. How are your organic search results compared with your competitors for generic keywords that apply to companies and products in your category?

9. What will you do to improve your search rankings for both generic and specific keywords?

10. Do vertical search engines offer unique value to your company?

*   Special thanks to Kraig Smith for his contribution to this chapter

Chapter 5

Social networks: Participant media and your business success

"Social Networking is the natural next step in Internet development. . . . Social networks allow people to assemble or allow computers to self-assemble connections that matter." Venture Capitalist Tim Draper

A global study conducted by Universal McCann in March 2008 involving 17,000 Internet users in 29 countries found that 58 percent of global Internet users are members of a digital community.[84] So, what exactly are digital communities or social networks? How have they become ubiquitous and what does their user base look like? More importantly, are they relevant for your business and if so, how?

Here are the basics. A social network within our context is a virtual community in cyberspace where members gather to communicate, organize, get introduced to others, seek and offer advice on everything from products and services to career transitions to fundraising for favorite causes.

Despite the recent explosion and adoption of social networks, they have existed in some form since 1997. According to Boyd and Ellison in 2007, the first attempt to create a true network was SixDegrees.com, which allowed users to create profiles, list their friends and look at their friends' lists.[85] In that sense, it was a true network because once you were in it, you could connect to others who you may not have known directly but with whom you could connect through your friends. The name SixDegrees.com, of course, had its genesis in the 1967 six degrees of separation theory proposed by sociologist Stanley Milgram who posited that that anyone around the world can be connected to any other person on the planet through a chain of acquaintances that has no more than five or six intermediaries.

From this concept sprung hundreds of social networks around the world. The most prominent ones in the U.S. today are Facebook, MySpace, LinkedIn and Bebo. QQ dominates the Chinese market while Orkut is prominent in Brazil and India. Mixi, Grono, Hyves, and Cyworld are some of the other lesser known but active networks around the world. You can expect to see many more segmented type of social networks popping up, e.g. enthusiasts of California wines.

The virtual communities are made up of people who willingly join and share information about themselves and their opinions. It is a marketer's dream landscape! The network sites parallel communities in the real world with two important exceptions. First, in the real world, one would have a hard time meeting and *remaining engaged* with such large numbers of people from around the world. Second, social networks uniquely take advantage of *strong and weak ties*. Strong ties form among our closest associates, while weak ties are diffused over various categories of association, e.g. someone you met at a conference.[86] Although both types of ties are important, research suggests weak ties may matter more under certain circumstances such as gathering information about which car we should drive or which social cause we should support. Ultimately, these online communities derive their power from the strength of the individuals who belong to them.

From a strategic business perspective, online communities have value and potential beyond cyber-gossiping or posting personal pictures and videos. In fact, social networks inspire a host of uses from the altruistic to commercial. They have become clearinghouses for sharing product, event, and service information; swapping resources; organizing and discussing political and social issues. And, they have opened up new worlds to individuals who are living in remote areas or are housebound.

Social networks have truly transformed how we communicate and relate to others; how we create, grow and strengthen alliances; and how these alliances are used to support causes, ideas, and interests. In essence, social networks have emerged not merely as communication tools for a generation of technology-savvy users but also as organizing, planning, fundraising, job-seeking and niche-marketing channels for average citizens as well as corporations, and community and not-for-profit organizations. The Universal McCann report suggests that social networks have evolved into *social utilities*. The growth and ubiquity of social networks is evident in the marketplace—and more and more in the business world. Social Networks are participant media tools that offer great potential for surfing the rift.

Are you LinkedIn?

Looking for a job? Seeking a new challenge in life or a new direction in business? Social networks are at the forefront of getting you there or helping you figure it out. Statistics confirm that social networks are not a passing fad. Around the world, several hundred million people actively use social networks on a regular basis. Researchers also found global penetration of social networks increasing, particularly in emerging markets.[87] As of May 2009, LinkedIn claimed to have a network of "more than 40 million experienced professionals from more than 200 countries around the world."[88] LinkedIn members list their professional data, share professional ideas and resources, and link to professional colleagues—both weak and strong ties. Thousands more joined LinkedIn as job hunters using connections to find company contacts and scope out company cultures without ever meeting their connection in person. Also as of May 2009, Facebook claimed more than 200 million active users, at least half of whom log in every day.[89] According to Web measurement service Alexa.com, Facebook is the fourth most-visited Web site in the U.S. and the top most visited of social networks alone.[90] Use of these sites skyrocketed beginning with the Fall 2008 economic downturn as many people were searching for new jobs, customers, old friends, volunteer opportunities, and ways to fill their free time after being laid off.

How viable are these social networking sites from a financial perspective? Facebook was valued at $15 billion when Microsoft acquired a 1.6% stake in the company in 2007. So, there is reason to believe that social networking offers more than "a bunch of college kids sharing photos of drinking parties and trying to hook up with each other."[91]

An online Harris Poll conducted March 31 and April 1, 2009, found that nearly half (48 percent) of adult Americans have either a Facebook or MySpace account, and 16 percent of adults update their social network pages at least daily. According to the Harris poll, however, the demographics still show a higher percentage usage among young adults (74 percent adoption of Facebook or MySpace among adults aged 18-34) than among older population segments (for example, 24 percent adoption of Facebook or MySpace among those 55 and older).[92]

Social networks provide access to large communities that share many common traits; are actively engaged in their digital world; and listen to opinions, ideas, and concerns of others. These digital communities offer online niches for companies that understand how to use them effectively. As they continue to grow, they will impact everything from business models to the future of communication.

Social networks and marketing

From a purely business perspective, why should your firm be involved in social networks? It's all about making connections and keeping those connections engaged—the driving force of participant media. Networks provide businesses access to and engagement with community members that share valuable characteristics. Viewed from a segmentation perspective, these communities are clusters of people that share many demographic and psychographic characteristics. When designed effectively (e.g., networks that offer resources and information to participants), they offer businesses significant benefits and opportunities to connect with a large segment of their target market.

Described below are several reasons why social networks are increasingly important to business:

- Social networks are large and getting larger. Jupiter Research estimates that by the year 2010 there will be 600 million people actively participating in social networks. These people, of course, are also prospective customers for a wide variety of products and services. Depending upon the structure, size, and strength of a particular network, businesses can engage these communities for a variety of purposes.

- Social networks are active. What makes people on social networks particularly attractive to marketers is the fact that most participants in these networks are not mere observers—they are active and engaged. They belong to these networks by choice. Once there, they share their experiences about ideas, people, products and things. Through cyber ties, this information is shared across a wide spectrum of people that pay attention to what is being said. We posit that "information elites" on many of these networks are sought after for their knowledge, and they have the power to significantly influence network participants.

- Social networks are clearinghouses of information and opinion. Social networks are significant by another key measure. According to a research by Fox Interactive Media, 40 percent of social network participants report they use social networking sites to learn more about brands or products; and 28 percent report a friend has recommended a brand or product to them via a social network.[93] Another study confirmed that social media can enhance or damage the reputation of a brand. It notes that 34 percent of social media users post opinions about products and brands.[94] Because these opinions are unfiltered and peer-to-peer directed, they may have a higher level of credibility than company-sponsored information.

- Social networks are relatively inexpensive places to advertise. According to eMarketer, companies had budgeted significant advertising resources to online communities for 2009. Much of this advertising, 70 percent, was expected to appear on the two most popular networks—MySpace and Facebook—where opinions are shared freely and frequently.[95]

- Social networks are unique. Users of social networks have integrated these sites into their daily routines. For example, more than half the active users of Facebook return to the site once daily and spend about 20 minutes each time updating information about themselves and their activities.[96] Few other media can claim this level of active participation, data access and engagement.

- Social media communities are varied. As noted earlier, while the very large networks dominate the social media landscape, numerous smaller social networks serve important niche markets. At least one social network seems to exist for every plausible interest and cause, for example, Fuzzster.com is a social network just for dog and cat owners. Most of the larger social networks have sub-groups devoted to issues, interests, and opinions. As engagement with social networks increases, so does the opportunity for marketers to showcase products, ideas and services. BBC News, reported that social networking sites "rather than acting as a glorified friend finder" are doing a lot more.[97] The recent addition of blood-type data on Facebook, which allows tracking of potential blood donors, ably demonstrates this.

- Social networks are effective because they are based on consumer-to-consumer content. As media fragmentation continues, consumers become increasingly fickle. They are less likely to respond to brand messages delivered through traditional mass media where marketers create and control content. People are learning from their personal networks how to gather product and service information. Sites such as Qype, Brownbook and Trustedplaces are acting as local and national business directories that share common social networking features.

- Social networks are easy to use and keep current. Participating in social networks requires no proprietary technology, nor any special technological or management skills. Nor does it require capital investment. In fact, social networks offer a level playing field in which small businesses may participate as effectively as large organizations. And, unlike traditional media, social networks are dynamic and nimbly respond to changing needs of their members.

- Social networks provide global access. While overall participation in social networks is increasing all over the world, consumers in many emerging markets are even more aggressive in their social network participation. For example, Universal McCann found that in the Philippines, more than 80 percent of Internet users belong to a social network as compared to roughly 50 percent of U. S. Internet users.

- Social networks are fun. Apart from the huge business potential of social networks, they work because they are fun. Network members have access to an expansive number of people in rural areas, towns and cities around the world. They can learn about each other without ever meeting face to face. Fun is the primary fuel driving most of the growth of social networks.

Social networking that works

All social networks are not created equal nor do they provide the same level of opportunities for businesses. Socially organized networks solicit broad audiences. Facebook, MySpace, and Orkut are some of the most successful sites used primary for socialization purposes, albeit they have branched out to special interest groups. LinkedIn, Visible Path, Ecademy, and Xing focus more on professional networking. Then there are "passion-centric" networks like Catster (for cat lovers, of course), AlwaysOn (technophiles), and Last.fm (music lovers). Activist networks such as Takepart.com address social issues; Couchsurfing.org connects travelers around the world; and MyChurch.org connects Christian churches and their members from around the world. In essence, there are social networks for almost every interest group and any age.

As these networks have become more sophisticated, they also have incorporated other enabling features to make the networking experience more fun and engaging. For example, Flickr (photo sharing), Last.fm (music listening habits), and YouTube (video sharing) have become integrated into various networks that expand their audiences.

True, these networks are fun and provide access to like-minded people but are they really productive from a business perspective? Does it make sense for your business to participate in a social network? Despite sometimes limited or hard-to-define marketing metrics for social network members, businesses have to remember that social networks have a very significant role in the lives of their users. Savvy companies see the potential in social media but are also acutely aware of how one wrong move can negate a lot of goodwill.

We've found some examples to share with you of companies that use social networks for a variety of objectives, from direct sales to creating a buzz about an event or new product. These examples illustrate that social networks offer all companies—large and small, business-to-business, and business-to-consumer—the opportunity to connect with their audiences.

Target, the big-box retailer for the masses, initially used social networking by sponsoring a page on Facebook as part of its back-to-school campaign. Target's Facebook page was geared to college dorm life and survival strategies for living with strangers. Its content featured member comments that ranged from the mundane, like suggestions for cooking with "dorm refrigerator" ingredients, to personality tests tied to dorm room furniture. The site also helped members upload and swap pictures of their dorms. Apart from a logo and a subtle "sponsored by" tag, the site looked like any regular social networking site. The response was quite impressive—the Target Facebook group had a membership of more than 7,000 within a month and generated 37 discussion sub-groups. Target deliberately kept the commercial nature of the site low key. so that when a Target ad appeared on Facebook, it was linked to Target's Facebook page, not to the mega e-commerce site for Target shopping.[98] Today, Target has several Facebook pages including Target Retail with more than 140,000 fans.

U.S.-based consumer product companies that have used social networking successfully include Disney,[99] Verizon,[100] Blockbuster,[101] AT&T,[102] Coca Cola,[103] Carnival Cruise,[104] and Proctor & Gamble.[105] Disney placed teasers on MySpace to effectively promote its movies, *Step Up* and *Step Up 2.* In both cases, the site offered the audience a chance to interact with the movies' director and stars. Disney also posted contests that gave members a chance to appear in a company event. This subtle marketing approach created an active engagement with the community that not only helped build brand awareness but also created word-of-mouth buzz for the movies. Research showed that more people saw the ad for the movie on MySpace than the original movie site (49 percent versus 37 percent) and the recall for ads on MySpace was significantly higher (58 percent) for people with a MySpace profile relative to those without a profile (26 percent). Why? Perhaps because people visiting MySpace were more focused due to the self-directed nature of their involvement in MySpace and less competition for their attention.

Verizon's social networking applications include customized ring tones and text messaging. Coca Cola has used its social networking site to hold contests that allowed users to design new vending machines. Sprite has created an application called Sprite Sips that allows users to customize a robotic Sprite character and add it to their site. This cleverly created site connected social networking with product sales by requiring the use of codes found only under Sprite beverage bottle caps to unlock special features in these robots.

Blockbuster.com uses its Facebook page to let users share titles of movies they've added to their queues. Carnival Cruise's social networking page allows people to discuss their travel experiences and review its cruises. Novice users are encouraged to connect with experienced cruisers and get tips. Passengers booked on upcoming trips can connect with their future shipmates before the cruise, creating trip-specific communities.

Companies also use multiple social networks specifically to promote their brands. AT&T promoted one of its global mobile phones on a social network for international travelers called WAYN.com ("Where are you now?").[106] Mars and Proctor & Gamble have used social networks not only to create a buzz around their products and promotions but also to sell products online. Procter & Gamble's social network is open only to those who have a personal

P&G e-mail account, making users feel part of the company's mission. The company uses its social networks for everything from recruiting employees to product testing, which allows the company to track members usage patterns. Unilever uses its site to test ad campaigns and market its products.

In addition to promoting products and brands, social networks to varying degrees have also been used to recruit potential job candidates, build and sustain employee relationships. Microsoft[107] and Starbucks[108] look to these networks to recruit. Goldman Sachs[109] and Deloitte[110] have their own online alumni networks to enlist former workers and cultivate future prospects for the company. Firms such as Intuit and MINIUSA have used customer networks to build brand loyalty and start passionate and convincing conversations about the brand.

Companies also use digital communities that exclusively serve the B2B market, not-for-profits and service firms. Not-for-profit and advocacy organizations such as The Humane Society of the United States,[111] American Heart Association,[112] World Wild Life Fund,[113] Oxfam International,[114] and Kiva[115] all have a strong presence on the Web and in many social networks. These communities generate conversations about social justice, the environment, health information and cause-related movements. Their dedicated supporters find these sites a central forum to voice ideas, express opinions and show support.

Tips for creating effective social networks

What are the best social networks for your organization? Here are some ideas to consider.

- Understand your target audience. How prevalent is its use of social networking? Are its needs best served by one or multiple networks? What makes this an effective way to connect with your audience?

- Assess your business goals for the community you seek to create and evaluate the core motivators for the audience you are targeting.

- Investigate how weak and strong connections operate in a particular network. Strong connections are people you know directly, weak connections or ties are people you connect with through others. Research in the social sciences has demonstrated that weak ties are crucial linkages to sustaining and growing networks. Examine the nature of ties and assess whether influencers and thought leaders in a network can affect outcomes. When possible, form alliances with thought leaders and influencers.

- Give members a reason to participate in a community. As noted earlier, research on social networks suggests that people use these communities for a reason such as information sharing or resource sharing, and they need an incentive to participate on an ongoing basis. In other words, ask yourself whether you offer them anything they can use in their daily lives. Give them a reason to connect with you and then engage them in several ways to create an enduring relationship with a community whose members value your organization and your brand.

- The primary driver for social network communities is member interaction. Communities foster multiple levels of interactions among members. Some are frequent and ongoing. Others may be sporadic. Encouraging and facilitating member interaction will keep the community vibrant and help it grow. This interaction also will provide valuable data in the form of member likes and dislikes, wants and needs.

- One of the primary reasons some businesses may still be reluctant to participate in social network communities is lack of control over content. Assess whether your organization is willing to give up some content control and whether organizational culture will support this change. Further, organizations must weigh the disadvantages of giving up control with the advantages that come from member feedback and engagement. Trying too hard to manage a community can backfire, as members may leave the community or publicly criticize the organization.

- Be prepared for negative feedback and comments. A campaign might not go as planned. Community members may start an unflattering buzz about your place, event or product. It is important for companies to be willing to accept criticism and to manage negative buzz into constructive feedback. Use criticism as an opportunity to improve business practices, engage the critics and demonstrate that the company is willing to take corrective measures.

- Communities always seek resources that make participation meaningful for them. Companies should offer tools that are both useful and innovative enough to create a good buzz. Uniquely useful tools can go viral—meaning they are passed around and talked about in the community.

- Offer an appealing overall experience. The sounds, the sights and the content surrounding the community should be compelling enough for the participants to keep coming back for more. Additionally, keep the content current, concise, and relevant to members.

- Offer value to community participants. Use contests, game, coupons, free shipping and other compelling opportunities to engage and reengage the community.

- Address member concerns and pay close attention to their requests. Content on social networks, such as user surveys, can be a great source of random market research.

- Keep communities dynamic. Online communities are constantly evolving just like land-based communities. Be flexible and offer dynamic content based upon audience preference.

- Vigilantly protect member privacy and monitor for inappropriate content. State your privacy policy clearly on your Web site. Violations of member trust are serious issues within online communities. Such infractions can cause serious harm to the brand.

- Ensure that your presence on these communities is not overly commercial and does not overshadow other more intrinsic uses of the community. Overtly commercial attempts may be viewed suspiciously by your audience driving them away and even generating negative buzz.

Companies must recognize that much of participant media, including social networks, symbolizes a fundamental shift in models of communication and marketing. Interaction on these social networks mirrors social interaction in the real world, in that much of it is unscripted and spontaneous. Marketing to individuals in these networks has to be different, subtle, and engaging. Users of social networks want to engage with providers, not be marketed to. They will decide what and when they want to hear, see and watch. In that sense, this new participant media communication model is democratic and organic. It also encompasses the essence of the word communication—from the Latin word *communis* meaning common thought. Companies that can master this new media model of marketing and communication will thrive on social networks to find new market segments and revenue streams

Action items

Here are action items for you to consider.

1. See how many of your customers and business associates you can find on LinkedIn, Facebook and Twitter.

2. Select ten clients and colleagues randomly and ask them what kind of value they are getting from social networking.

3. Discuss with your co-workers which social networking site they think will offer your company the most value.

Ten questions

Now ask yourself the following questions.

1. Do you have an account on any of the social networking sites? Do you use it for business or personal communications?

2. How do you consider social networking personally relevant to you?

3. Does your company currently use social networking as part of its overall business communications strategy?

4. If so, which sites are you using and why?

5. Who is responsible for managing your company's social networking presence and measuring its effectiveness?

6. Do you think social networking in your industry makes sense?

7. Do you see any evidence of your competitors using social networking strategically?

8. What organizational or cultural barriers at your company limit the effectiveness of social networking?

9. Does your company encourage employees to engage in social networking as an aspect of their jobs?

10. Do you see any downside to your company's use of social networking?

Chapter 6

Collaboration: The power of online communication

> "Instead of looking to a single person for the right answers, companies need to recognize a simple truth: Under the right conditions, groups are smarter than the smartest person within them." James Surowiecki, *The Wisdom of Crowds*[116]

Participant media tools may have the greatest impact on business in the area of collaboration and how we all work together. This is a rift we should all be surfing by working effortlessly with our remote colleagues and customers without ever leaving our offices or homes. One of the most powerful capabilities of participant media technologies is the ability to collaborate online to create new and more useful knowledge. The building block of this phenomenon is the idea that collective intelligence provides superior ability to produce knowledge more efficiently and effectively.

In his book, *Crowdsourcing*, Jeff Howe wrote, "Far more important and interesting are the human behaviors technology engenders, especially the potential of the Internet to weave the mass of humanity together into a thriving, infinitely powerful organism."[117] The democratization of technology is where people believe in the power of many to create something that is of benefit to many. The new generation of technology users has come to expect information sharing as the norm rather than the exception. This desire to contribute and collaborate with others has fueled technologies including Web conferencing, virtual worlds, instant messaging, and wikis that have made the world a smaller place. Collaborative tools such as wikis and virtual worlds bring together diverse groups of people to create and distribute knowledge in ways once thought impossible but now are increasingly vital.

In a lecture at the Massachusetts Institute of Technology, Cisco Chairman and CEO John Chambers defined collaboration as "co-labor working together for a common goal." He went on to describe Web 2.0 as "networked technologies that enable collaboration." Web 2.0 is truly interactive and collaborative, and encourages participation, community building, and feedback.[118]

Web conferencing

Although Web conferences and Webinars have been around for a number of years, widespread adoption and increased functionality make these technologies a key collaborative tool today. Webex,[119] Live Meeting,[120] Go To Meeting,[121] Adobe Connect,[122] and others have become mainstays of many sales, marketing, conferencing, training, and customer support efforts. As travel becomes more expensive and cumbersome, companies want more efficient ways to connect with their vendors and customers. Sales people use Web conferencing and Webcasts to conduct sales presentations, offer product demonstrations, and connect with clients on a variety of matters. Firms also use Webinars to reach and inform groups of prospects, employees, and other stakeholders. So, while these technologies are not completely new, companies continue to find innovative uses for them. More importantly, these technologies have become more powerful and, they increasingly occupy a more central role in a company's integrated marketing communications strategy. Clearly, these technologies aren't meant to replace all human, face-to-face interactions, nevertheless, they are effectively replacing many face-to-face meetings.

For example, Stream57,[123] a Webcasting site, enables businesses to customize their Webcasting efforts, offering users access to virtual events where they can reach speakers and key opinion leaders from any broadband-equipped location around the world. Recent technologies allow multiple users from multiple locations to appear and interact seamlessly, without any interruption or lag. A company can host a live event in which panelists from around the globe can discuss their opinions and bring ideas to an audience that may be located anywhere in the world. With text, audio and video capabilities, these meetings deliver the same information as a live meeting, without anyone having to leave the office.

There are several ways in which companies and individuals can use Web conferencing technologies. You could, for example, use a customized Webcast to deliver your trade show presentation to potential buyers from around the world who may otherwise have had to travel long distances and incur expenses. Or perhaps you have a new product announcement that your vendors are eagerly awaiting. You may want to train a national sales team for a new product launch or discuss company strategy with a dispersed management team. These tools allow you to bring in everyone without the expense and time loss of distance travel.

Some of the new technologies are so powerful that the platform does not even have to be company owned. In other words, you don't have to worry about browser or platform issues that may interfere with the quality of delivery. Companies can contract with vendors to use these tools to network, meet vendors, and learn from others, in real time, but in virtual place. Additionally, with instant messaging (IM) and online chat tools, you can avoid other costly and cumbersome interactions.

Skype[124] is a low-cost platform for video phone calls and conferences as well as other digital telephony services. Globally, Skype has become an important tool for the broadcast news media that use the service as a means for filing stories from remote locations. Internet news programs such as "Freedom Watch" on FoxNews.com use Skype to interview guests from remote locations. The availability of Skype and similar applications remove most if not all of the technological and financial barriers that have prevented businesses from incorporating live video into their communications strategies.

Wiki

> "Wikis harness the wisdom of crowds, serving as virtual commons where participants can wrestle over ideas and information until something approaching consensus—or the truth—emerges."
> *Harvard Business Review*[125]

Thousands of organizations from Microsoft to the FBI use wikis to aggregate the knowledge of their far-flung employees, creating a place for them to electronically converge and collaborate on everything from planning meetings and documenting best practices to brainstorming about new products and processes. A wiki is a Web site that allows visitors to make changes, contributions, or corrections. These sites are used for collaboration and the most widely know is Wikipedia, the online encyclopedia. Good wikis are not merely random collections of information—a good wiki must have information that is otherwise hard to find or does not exist elsewhere.

The strength of wikis is not the simple act of collaboration but the aggregation of knowledge by experts who are able and willing to share what they know and are passionate about ensuring that the knowledge is not merely shared but preserved.

Wikis are rapidly becoming a collaborative tool of choice for many corporations. The software giant SAP has many uses for wikis. A community of expert project managers, business process architects, application consultants and other business process professionals contribute to SAP wikis, which have evolved to include interest areas ranging from enterprise resource planning to customer relationship management. According to SAP, there are now at least "18 industry-focused communities within SAP."[126] Clearly, the existence of these wikis attests to the power of shared knowledge and the interest in such knowledge. Here are some of the reasons a wiki may provide your organization strategic value:

- Wikis can be the heart of any knowledge base from the highly technical to the entertaining. Research and collaborative knowledge can be used to support products and services as well as generate buzz and interest in a product or service, as amply demonstrated by wikis for network television programs such as *CSI*.

- A wiki's success derives from the power of collective intelligence. Individuals with a passion for a topic may create a wiki to share thoughts with others who share that interest. The Tolkien Wiki for fans of author J. R. R. Tolkien, and The Open Guide to London wiki, for travelers to that great city are good examples of specialized wikis.[127] Wikis can accept contributions from within and outside an organization or group. The cumulative impact of all the collaborators will in most cases result in a whole that is greater than the sum of its parts.

- Wikis are an easy and relatively inexpensive tool to create information and knowledge, which you can share globally with anyone—customers, colleagues and strangers alike. Wikis are an easy way to contribute and edit information in real time. In addition, graphics and video can be embedded on the pages consolidating all elements of a project in one place that can be accessed by all interested parties.

- Wikis can serve as a replacement or supplement for corporate Intranets. Corporate Intranets typically consist of informational documents on the company such as newsletters, phone directories, procedural forms and policies.

- Because they are created by users, wikis make it possible to keep the information current and relevant without taxing internal resources.

Advantages and disadvantages of a wiki

Clearly the biggest advantage of a wiki is that it harnesses the *wisdom of groups of people*. The power of collective knowledge is the cornerstone of good wikis. People are passionate about what they know and are more likely to read other people's ideas on subjects that most matter to them. When knowledge is generated from other users who are experts in their fields, the motivation to share is higher than when a single individual is tasked to produce information.

Wikis are mostly self correcting. When Wikipedia was first launched, users feared that information integrity would be compromised since anyone wanting to contribute to a subject matter could do so, without a required depth of knowledge on a particular subject. Another big concern was that wiki contributors would produce unregulated and biased information. However, evidence suggests that communities, particularly volunteer communities are not merely zealous about sharing information but also sharing the most accurate information. Inaccurate and biased information produced by one can be, and is, corrected by others equally passionate about ensuring the integrity of information.

Wikis can foster interaction and build strong connections among your customers. Visualize an environment where customers can share their knowledge about the products and services that your company provides. They can be your firm's most loyal advocates and can share positive information on the performance of a product or service. Blogs can also do this to some extent, but wikis can offer this information in a more integrated manner.

When a wiki is used as an internal company communication vehicle to provide updates on the company's progress and programs, it encourages open communication among employees. The fact that the company wiki is user-generated makes it more likely that people will actually read the information and will view it as more honest.

Wikis have certain disadvantages. If information is inaccurate, subjective, and not monitored, the wiki may lose credibility. However, this challenge is no different than any other participant media. The key is to have broad participation from active and passionate users who value information sharing. Wikis won't work if individuals are driven by motives other than information sharing. What makes a wiki powerful—open collaboration—also leaves it vulnerable to sabotage.

In some organizations, users may have trouble accepting wikis. If an organization does not foster open communication, a wiki may be hard to sustain. This may be especially true in companies that equate access to information with power. These organizations and individuals may view a wiki as directly challenging their influence, as information access migrates from a select few to the many. When the information environment in a company becomes democratic, some people may feel uncomfortable and not necessarily agree with this dissipation of power that controlled information access provided them. However, this is an issue relating to organizational culture and not necessarily a limitation of wikis. Further, in organizations where information has traditionally been transmitted hierarchically and where a culture of empowerment is not fostered, people may not willingly contribute to a wiki. Of course, as with any other open medium, companies have to be vigilant that the information shared is accurate and not designed to drive an agenda.

Virtual worlds

Less than five years ago if someone had mentioned the term Second Life®, the reaction most likely would not been a vision of a three-dimensional digital environment mimicking the real world! Yet, today, Second Life is one of the many computer-simulated environments, called virtual worlds, inhabited by digital representations of people and objects, where digital interactions replace or supplement live interactions and where people can conduct transactions including buying and selling "virtual" property. From a purely entertainment perspective, virtual worlds such as Second Life can give you a kind of second life. You can be anyone you want to be through your alter ego and thrive in a digital representation of the world you always wanted.

In a virtual world, representations of people are referred to as avatars (derived from Sanskrit to mean descent from a supreme being to a more mortal form created for special purposes). Avatars interact with each other and behave in a fashion very similar to what they would do in the real world including cultural nuances that may drive their real world behavior. Your avatar can transport to various locations where your company has virtual presence. For example, your avatar can interact with vendors in one meeting room and then fly to another where a strategy session is taking place among co-workers from around the world.

To many this idea of creating a simulated identity in a simulated world may sound childish and best suited for creating a fantasy world purely for entertainment purposes. Virtual worlds are indeed used for gaming and entertainment purposes. Massively multiplayer online role-playing games (MMORPGs) such as World-of-Warcraft, and massively multiplayer online real-life games (MMORLGs) are among the popular forms of virtual games using pre-existing or self-created avatars. However, virtual worlds are equally effective in offering real world business solutions as discussed in the following examples.

Numerous companies have a virtual world presence. More than 1,300 companies participated in the 2008 Virtual Worlds Expo held in Los Angeles, and the 2009 Virtual Worlds Expo slated to be held in New York includes participants as diverse as IBM, Mattel and MTV.[128] Companies such as Nike, Sony, Sears, Men's Warehouse, NBC, Sun, Adidas, Toyota and Dell maintain a presence on Second Life, attesting to the growing importance of virtual worlds. According to IBM, "We see the incredible potential for the 3-D Internet to transform end user experiences, improve business processes and to impact innovation across business, government and society."[129]

There are two types of virtual worlds: Open and private. Open virtual worlds, such as Second Life, are accessible to the public and have, in some cases, millions of members. This large membership represents both a huge market and a security risk. You cannot control what happens in these worlds since anyone with the right technology can participate and be part of an open virtual world. Private virtual worlds, on the other hand, limit participants and control. Generally this approach is more expensive and does not offer the interaction with outsiders that open environments foster. Proton Media is a company that offers such closed virtual world environments.

A report titled "Getting Work Done in Virtual Worlds" by Forester Research details how virtual worlds like Second Life and There.com are increasingly becoming mainstream business tools.[130] Virtual World tools can be used for remote training, collaboration and creation with participants from almost anywhere in the world. Here are but a few examples of how organizations can use virtual world technologies.

Remote collaboration

In a global economy, competencies and challenges cross political and geographic boundaries. Your experts don't need to be confined to one central office. In 2002, IBM Haifa, Fraunhofer SIT of Germany, and five other European Union companies started their partnership to develop what they appropriately termed UNITE—a Ubiquitous and Integrated Teamwork Environment. The effort included such diverse areas as graphic design provided by a Portuguese company; business models from Fraunhofer IAO of Germany; project requirements and product dissemination managed by a French company; and IBM Haifa contributed communication and collaboration middleware.

With more powerful technologies today, the ability to create and cooperate in the virtual world is attracting more business users. Think about a virtual world, where avatars from all corners of the world can interact in the same virtual room for idea generation, product design, development and dissemination. According to the Forester report, "In a virtual meeting room, you can see who is present; who is multi-tasking; who has raised a hand; or who has been away from their keyboard so long that their avatar has fallen asleep." Not only does this minimize the costs of bringing experts to one physical location, it can create a much livelier collaborative environment than a physical one!

Experiential learning

Your employees can learn new skills in a virtual environment by taking on the avatar of someone else and experiencing their world. A sales executive can inhabit the world of a product developer to gain a better understanding of the product capabilities. Think how much more effective such experience is than merely participating in a product presentation. In the virtual world, you *can* walk in someone else's shoes. Imagine the difference between learning about diversity in a classroom and being the minority individual or someone with restricted ability challenges that lives in a prejudiced world. Virtual worlds can teach someone to be more understanding and empathetic by navigating in an unfamiliar environment. Indeed, navigating challenges in the virtual world by mimicking some of the real world can offer a new way of disseminating corporate values, policies and strategies. Compared to traditional classroom instruction, training in a virtual world can offer substantial savings, enhance retention, and provide all employees a view into other people's work lives. Customized virtual world training can reflect experiences that are most powerful and most relevant to the individual undergoing training.

Coaching and mentoring

"War is no game, of course, but games, in a big way, have updated war," noted a 2006 *Washington Post* article that described how the U.S. Army trains soldiers for combat. The Army considers virtual world training necessary in the face of ever more sophisticated weapons and enemies in more hostile, remote environments.[131]

Virtual environments are perfect for coaching and mentoring in a wide array of disciplines. Whether you are a surgeon who needs coaching to perform a difficult operation in a remote location or a soldier who needs training in maneuvering new battleground technology, avatars can deliver needed information, effectively offering visual representations of the actual process and letting you learn as you go by participating in it.

Duke University collaborates with Virtual Heroes, Inc., to create a virtual environment for training healthcare workers in teamwork and communication skills.[132] Princeton University uses a three-dimensional virtual world to manage distributed teams for a large-scale astrophysics project. The University of Maryland uses it to simulate highway emergencies. Yale University, The Johns Hopkins University, National Naval Medical Center and Tufts University collaboratively develop training environments to help medical professionals practice decision-making and experience-based skills in a virtual hospital setting.[133]

Sales presentations and virtual trade shows

> "The beauty of virtual trade shows is that they are, well, virtual.
> That makes them not only cheap but entirely flexible, with formats
> ranging from a basic online directory of companies and products
> to an eye-popping Web site with virtual booths—detailed right
> down to the curtain designs and smiling cyber-greeters, a la the
> meta-world Second Life."[134] *Forbes* magazine

Recruiting

Perhaps it comes as no surprise that in a global marketplace, employee
talent is dispersed worldwide and competition for this talent is often fierce.
Companies competing in the global economy need to recruit, train, and
retain individuals who can function productively and effectively in this
setting. Virtual environments offer an excellent platforms to showcase
a company, offer information on the opportunities available and invite
potential employees for job interviews.

Action items

Here are action items for you to consider.

1. Take an inventory of the collaborative technologies and applications that your company uses today.

2. Ask five customers how their companies are using collaborative technologies.

3. Discuss with your colleagues how your company could improve or accelerate its adoption and use of collaborative technologies.

Ten questions

Now ask yourself the following questions.

1. Who needs to collaborate in your organization?

2. How are you doing it today?

3. Are there training situations that can benefit from virtual worlds?

4. What are the best ways to collaborate with partners and customers?

5. How have you personally used collaboration technologies on the job?

6. Who is responsible for planning and implementing the use of collaboration technologies and applications in your company?

7. Have you tested and selected your collaboration platforms?

8. Are your customers using collaboration technologies? Do they expect you to be able to use the same technologies in working with them?

9. Do any organizational or cultural considerations impede your company's effective use of collaboration technologies?

10. How important are collaboration technologies to your company's continued growth, competitiveness, and success?

Chapter 7

Final thoughts: You can be surfing today's rifts and anticipating the next big wave!

We began this book by introducing the concept of rifts or shifts in the landscape of business, technology and the economy. We posed a metaphorical challenge: Start surfing the rifts as a way to manage your response to seismic changes in our world. We identified the rifts and their causes: Generational differences in technology adoption; the weakening of traditional models such as "interruption marketing;" and the rapid evolution of Web 2.0 technologies. We shared with you some insights about understanding and adopting a variety of key platforms and technologies to help you start surfing, including blogs, video, podcasts, social networks, search engines, wikis and virtual worlds. We collectively titled these the new participant media.

So, now what do you do with this information?

First of all, you don't have to use all of these technologies immediately. Pick two or three technologies that offer the most relevant and immediate impact to your target markets and industry segment; then get comfortable with using them in your business; set measurable objectives; and monitor your results.

To help you get started, try following these suggestions:

- Research how your customers and competitors are using new media technologies. Learn from their successes and mistakes.

- Start with pilot programs for the technologies you choose to employ. Starting small will enable you to adjust quickly, see some results, and start building consensus. You're also more likely to find internal champions for each project.

- Enlist the participation of your tech-savvy employees. They already use most Web 2.0 technologies in their personal lives, and they can help build enthusiasm quickly for your initiatives.

- Bring in outside experts to help you define strategies, tactics and metrics. Finding the right consultant that has helped others with these issues will accelerate your program's implementation.

- Establish rules and define roles. Let people know how they can participate and what the limits are to their participation. Monitoring and enforcing the rules will spare you many problems down the road.

- Strive for consistency and stay current. If you're on Twitter, make sure you post relevant content daily or at least several times weekly, and be sure your links take readers to pages they will find useful. If you launch a group or company profile on Facebook or LinkedIn, monitor the content daily, provide engaging content every week, and participate in your group members' conversations with appropriate frequency.

- Secure senior management support. Remember, the benefits of these new technologies, applications and platforms may not be immediately evident to senior executives who are focused on other important aspects of your enterprise. You'll have to be a teacher, trainer, coach, and champion.

- Maintain openness and transparency with all of your internal and external constituencies. There's nowhere to hide on the Internet, and any attempt to operate in secrecy will inevitably result in a loss of trust and credibility that may be difficult, if not impossible, to regain.

- Monitor and modify your use of these technologies. If you're going to fail, it's better to fail fast, and move on to other solutions.

- Continue to review the action items and questions provided at the end of each chapter. They can help you formulate a plan and keep you on track to success.

Trends worth watching

As Web 2.0 technologies and platforms continue evolving into Web 3.0 and beyond, we expect to witness the emergence or acceleration of six vital trends within the sphere of participant media.

- Mobile convergence: This is a rapidly developing trend, as evidenced by the newest generation of mobile devices that take advantage of all-digital (3G and 4G) wireless networks to provide a robust combination of communications and data services. These devices let you take the world with you, no matter where you are going. Examples include the Apple iPhone 3GS, the Palm Pre, a variety of wireless notebook computers, and Amazon's Kindle. Global Positioning System (GPS) technology is an aspect of this convergence, adding a new level of geographical intelligence to mobile computing and communications. Vendors will continue refining this to achieve the "holy grail" of personal information technology—a single, compact device that acts as a phone, a computer, a camera, a voice recorder, a messaging system, a Web interface, an entertainment device, a location-sensitive "intelligent advisor," a video player, a game machine, a text reader and more—all at an affordable price.

- Cloud computing: This is the idea of Software-as-a-Service (SaaS) on steroids. Your software will reside in the cloud and not on your device (think G-mail). Software applications will undergo constant revisions and updates, a perpetual beta version that adds refinements continually. A book, a training manual or a piece of software will continually evolve. Instead of buying multiple versions of something over a period of time, you will have access to an ever-evolving version at all times. "We're seeing the rise of cloud computing, the vast array of interconnected machines managing the data and software that used to run on PCs," wrote Steve Hamm in *Business Week*. "(The) combination of mobile and cloud technologies are shaping up to be one of most significant advances in the computing universe in decades . . . Cloud computing means that information is not stranded on individual machines; it is combined into one digital 'cloud' available at the touch of a finger from many different devices."[135]

- Flat organizations and global collaboration: Collaboration and communication technologies will reduce our traditional reliance on organizational hierarchies. Author of the new book, *The Future Arrived Yesterday*, Michael Malone "predicts that technological advances will continue at an ever faster pace . . . An enterprise will do best when it features 'an amorphous external form,' adapting to markets, customers, competition, and even ownership as they change (which they inevitably will). No less important, it will evolve an 'internal center' that maintains 'the identity and continuity of the enterprise over time.'"[136]

- Ubiquitous video: The use of and reliance on video and audio will continue accelerating, while text will become a means of annotating multi-media presentations. Recall your first impression of YouTube; you're not alone if you thought it was a gimmick. But today, video is everywhere: Embedded into Web pages (soon to be embedded into email, as G-mail has begun testing a video-enabled version); available on several video-hosting services; emerging as staple technology for blogging and podcasting; and created by accessible and portable devices ranging from cell phones to studio-quality video cameras. Your customers will come to expect that you will present information in video format. Other key audiences, including employees and investors, will expect video delivery of important company announcements and updates. Video will become the preferred online technology, not only for news and entertainment, but for training and education, which brings us to our next trend.

- Just-in-time learning: Technology has played an important role in training and education during the past 30 years. The direction of this trend suggests that anyone will be able to use whatever technology platform best suits his or her learning style. And, the content will be made available on any device, any time, anywhere. Think of a book. Traditionally, reading a printed copy of the book was the only way to absorb its content. Now you have the choice of reading it on a Kindle or similar device; downloading chapters from a Web site to your computer or mobile device; listening on your iPod to an audio version read by the author or another narrator; delving into the book's content on a wiki (and adding your own commentary); and experiencing an online video presentation by the author. Apply those choices to training and education, and you can see that the power of online technologies will enable all styles and levels of learning, faster and more effectively than ever before.

"Today, our kids get their information from the Internet, downloaded onto their iPods, and in Twitter feeds to their cell phones," California Governor Arnold Schwarzenegger observed. "A world of up-to-date information fits easily into their pockets and onto their computer screens. So why California's public school students are still forced to lug around antiquated, heavy, expensive textbooks?"[137]

• Avatar-as-interface: In the new world of participant media, your avatar will be your three-dimensional interface to the Web world. The World Future Society describes Project Lifelike as "a consortium of university computer researchers funded by the National Science Foundation (that) aims to create visualizations specific to an individual, and combine those visualizations with sophisticated artificial intelligence that could also replicate the individual's responses."[138] Because of the frequently nonverbal nature of communications, avatars will accurately portray body language and subtle gestures. Avatars also will remember and learn from their encounters with live users, becoming ever more lifelike in their communication capabilities. Recall our discussion in the previous chapter of the use of avatars in training and human resource applications. The future applications of the use of avatars may be limited only by our imaginations.

Keeping pace with technology isn't easy but understanding and appreciating its potential can keep you ahead the competition and may provide an advantage. It's not only important to know what's available today but also what trends will impact the future. Monitor these trends and understand their implications—you'll be waves ahead of your competition in surfing tomorrow's rifts.

# # # # #

Epilogue

We recognize that the topic of this book is fluid in nature and large in scale—much like the business landscape in which we operate today. It would be impossible to include all current information on evolving new media in one guide. So, with this in mind and to get you this information in a timely way, we decided to release the first edition as an e-book in October, 2009. The hard cover and softcover editions were published later in 2009.

Most important, we encourage you and your co-workers to participate in an ongoing dialogue about participant media and its relevance to business and the marketplace. Is it the next wave? Or, are these tools just a trendy fad? Tell us what you think. Share your experiences, thoughts, ideas, and reactions. We live in the participant media world and want to open it up to our readers. Please visit our Web site at *www.surfingtherift.com* to join the conversation and to see real-time examples of what we cover in the book.

Glossary of Terms

Aggregators—software or Web applications that aggregate Web content such as news headlines, blogs, and podcasts in a single location for easy viewing.

Avatar—a representation of a computer user in the form of a three-dimensional figure, a two-dimensional picture, or object. The term can also refer to the personality connected with the screen name of an Internet user.

Blogs—a broad term referring to a Web site where people regularly write about a variety of topics.

Blogoshere—a term used to describe the belief that blogs exist together with interconnections as a community or social network.

Cloud computing—a style of computing in which technical capabilities are provided as a service, allowing users to generate complex technology related applications via the Internet (the cloud). Users are not required to have knowledge or expertise to create.

Facebook—was founded in 2004 and is a free-access social networking Web site that is operated and privately owned by Facebook, Inc.

Global Positioning System (GPS)—a satellite-based navigation system made up of a network of 24 satellites placed into orbit by the U.S. Department of Defense and used as tracking devices for all kinds of business and government applications.

Internet—a publicly accessible series of interconnected computer networks that transmit data worldwide by packet switching using the standard Internet Protocol (IP).

Intranet—a secure, private network shared by a group of users or an organization using the same type of protocols (TCP/IP) and software found on the public Intranet.

Interruption marketing—traditional form of marketing, particularly advertising, in which marketers designed, managed and controlled customized messages directed to individuals using mass media e.g. network television, radio and publications.

LinkedIn—a business-oriented social networking site mainly used for professional networking.

The long tail—a niche strategy used by businesses such as Netflix.com and Amazon.com. Unlike a regular store that holds the most popular items in inventory, these businesses stock low-demand products that a lot of people would buy since they can't get them anywhere else.

Mobile computing—a term describing the ability to use technology while in motion or transit, e.g. a smart phone or netbook.

MySpace—a social networking with an interactive, user-submitted network of friends, personal profiles, blogs, groups, photos, music, and videos.

Participant media—refers to online community-building sites, blogs and other Web tools are that skyrocketing in popularity and encouraging anyone with access to the World Wide Web to express their ideas, opinions, information, data, and questions.

Podcast—an audio broadcast that has been converted to an MP3 file or other audio format for playback on a digital music player. Even though they were developed for digital music players like an iPod, most podcasts are listened to on a computer.

Really Simple Syndication (RSS)—a group of Web-feed formats used to publish frequently updated works such as news headlines or blogs. More simply it helps the people producing this user-generated content do it more efficiently and quickly.

Search Engine Marketing (SEM)—a type of Internet marketing that promotes Web sites by increasing their visibility in search engine result pages through the use of paid placement, paid inclusion, and context advertising.

Search Engine Optimization (SEO)—is the process of improving the volume or quality of traffic to a Web site from search engines such as Google and Yahoo! by monitoring and manipulating natural, organic, algorithmic search results.

Semantic Web—computer intelligence to understand Web content

Social media—Internet-based tools for sharing and discussing information among human beings. Technologies used inside of it are blogs, picture-sharing, vlogs, wall-postings, e-mail, instant messaging, music-sharing, crowdsourcing, VOIP, and many more. Also referred to as new media.

Social networking sites—a Web site that provides a virtual community for people interested in a particular subject, ideas, or to just hang out together. Members create their own online profile with biographical data, pictures, and any other information they choose to post. They can communicate with each other in a variety of ways while never actually meeting in person.

Software as a Service (SaaS)—accessing software over the Internet instead of buying the software and installing it on your own computer.

Twitter—a free social networking and micro-blogging service that enables its users to send and read other users' updates known as tweets.

User-generated content—also known as consumer-generated media, is a term that originated in 2005 and refers to publicly available information created by Internet users.

Voice Over Internet Protocol (VOIP)—using the Internet to deliver voice communications (calls) instead of the public switched telephone network that is normally used.

YouTube—a video sharing Web site on which users can upload and share videos.

Viddler—a video sharing Web site on which users can upload and share videos.

Vodcast—shortened version of the term video podcast and refers to a podcast in a compressed movie format, often containing a combination of animation sequences, moving images and sound.

Widgets—objects on a computer screen that the user interacts with and uses to do certain tasks.

Web 2.0—a term used to describe the second wave of the Internet. It involves using the Web and its tools in a whole new way by having users generate content themselves rather than just viewing pages online. The term was first coined by O'Reilly Media in 2004.

Web 3.0—a superseding term to Web 2.0, which is highly speculative because the technologies that will be utilized in it are not yet invented. It is just another step in the evolution of the Internet.

Wiki—enables documents to be authored collectively in a simple language using a Web browser. "Wiki" means "super fast" in the Hawaiian language, and it is the speed of creating and updating pages that is a defining aspect of wiki technology.

World Wide Web—refers to information available on the Internet that can be easily accessed with software usually called a "browser." Organizations publish their information on the Web in a format known as HTML (or more recently in XML with an accompanying CSS or XSL style sheet). This information is usually referred to as their "home page" or "Web site." Also known as WWW or the Web.

Endnotes

Chapter 1

1 "How Companies Are Marketing Online: A McKinsey Global Survey," *McKinsey Quarterly,* September 2007.
2 "November 19-December 20, 2008 Tracking Survey," *Pew Internet & American Life Project,* Updated January 6, 2009.
3 "How Companies Are Marketing Online: A McKinsey Global Survey," *McKinsey Quarterly,* September 2007.
4 John Boudreau, "Smart Phones Serve As Constant Companion As New Apps Change How Mobile Devices Are Used," *RISMEDIA,* March 28, 2009.
5 Geoff Ramsey, "3 Hidden Trends in 2008," *eMarketer,* January 14, 2008.
6 Seth Godin, *Permission Marketing* (New York: Simon & Schuster, 1999." 29.
7 "Marketers Must Change How They Appeal to Consumers If They Want to Capitalize on Promise of New Media," *Business Wire,* April 18, 2005.
8 Jagdish N. Sheth, Rajendra S. Sisodia, *Does Marketing Need Reform?* (New York: M.E. Sharpe, 2006), 13.
9 Cate Riegner, "Word of Mouth on the Web: The Impact of Web 2.0 on Consumer Purchase Decisions," *Journal of Advertising Research,* 2007 v47 i4. 436-447.
10 "Marketers Must Change How They Appeal to Consumers If They Want to Capitalize on Promise of New Media," *Business Wire,* April 18, 2005.
11 "The New New Media: Global Lessons on the Future of Media, Content, and Messaging," *IBM Report,* 2007.
12 JetBlue YouTube Channel, *www.youtube.com/user/JetBlueCorpComm*

[13]   Steve Anderson, "Unless you are living in a cave, you can't help but notice the impact of, or at least the buzz about social networking sites," *The Automated Agency Report,* 2007.

[14]   Tim O'Reilly, "Design Patterns and Business Models for the Next Generation of Software," *www.oreilly.com,* September 30, 2005.

[15]   "November 19-December 20, 2008 Tracking Survey," *Pew Internet & American Life Project,* Updated January 6, 2009.

[16]   Amanda Lenhart, "Adults and Social Networking Web sites, *Pew Internet Project Data Memo,* January 14, 2009.

[17]   Charlene Li, "Social Technographics: Mapping Participation in Activities Forms The Foundation of a Social Strategy," *Forester Research,* April 19, 2007.

Chapter 2

[18]   "Inside the War Against China's Blogs," *BusinessWeek,* June 23, 2008.

[19]   The Mark Cuban Weblog, *blogmaverick.com.*

[20]   Technorati, *www.technorati.com.*

[21]   G. Marken, "To Blog or Not to Blog," *Public Relations Quarterly 2005,* 50(3), 31-33.

[22]   Jonathan Schwartz, "If You Want to Lead, Blog," *Harvard Business Review 2005,* 83(11), 30.

[23]   General Motors blog, *fastlane.gmblogs.com.*

[24]   Garmin blog, *garmin.blogs.com.*

[25]   "The New Digital Divide: How the Generation of Digital Consumers is Transforming Mass Communication," *Universal McCann Study,* 2006.

[26]   Nuts About Southwest, *www.blogsouthwest.com.*

[27]   Tom Peters blog, *www.tompeters.com.*

[28]   Charlene Li Groundswell blog, *blogs.forrester.com/groundswell.*

[29]   Guy Kawasaki blog: How to Change the World, *blog.guykawasaki.com.*

[30]   Seth Godin blog, *sethgodin.typepad.com.*

[31]   Tanuja Singh, Liza Verson-Jackson, Joe Cullinane, "Blogging: A New Play in Your Marketing Game Plan," *Business Horizons,* July-August 2008, V51, 268.

[32]   Sarah Perez, "How to Get Customer Service via Twitter," *Read Write Web,* April 10, 2008. (*www.readwriteWeb.com/archives/how_to_get_customer_service_via_twitter.php*)

[33] MommyCast, *www.mommycast.com.*

[34] Erik Sherman, "Out of Control," *Advertising Age,* April 3, 2006, 7(14), 9-12.

[35] Budget Car Rental blog, *www.upyourbudget.com.*

[36] Vespa Scooters blog, *www.vespascootersblog.com.*

[37] Ken Levy blog, *mashupx.com/blog.*

[38] "Oprah, Ashton Kutcher Mark Twitter 'Turning Point'," *CNN,* April 18, 2009.

[39] Steve Johnson, "How Twitter Will Change the Way We Live," *Time Magazine,* June 5, 2009.

[*] Thanks to Mary Murtaugh for the phrase 'word of thumbs"

[40] CNN Breaking News on Twitter, *twitter.com/cnnbrk.*

[41] Rick Sanchez on Twitter, *twitter.com/ricksanchezCnn.*

[42] Guy Kawasaki, "Looking for Mr. Goodtweet: How to Pick Up Followers on Twitter," *blog.guykawasaki.com,* November 10, 2008.

[43] Dell on Twitter, *twitter.com/dellOutlet.*

[44] John C. Abell, "Dude – Dell's Making Money Off Twitter," Wired, June 12, 2009.

[45] Matthew Fraser, Soumitra Dutta, "Yes, CEOs Should Facebook and Twitter," Forbes, March 11, 2009.

[46] NASA on Twitter, *twitter.com/nasa.*

[47] Jack and Suzy Welch, "Why We Tweet," *BusinessWeek,* June 2, 2009.

Chapter 3

[48] "CEO John Chambers Discusses Cisco's Q3 Performance," *EMS Now,* May 14, 2008.

[49] The Long Tail blog by Chris Anderson, *www.longtail.typepad.com/ the_long_tail.*

[50] Paul Verna, "Podcast Advertising: Seeking Riches in Niches," *eMarketer,* January 2008.

[51] "Public Radio Technology Survey," *Public Radio Program Directors Association,* 2008.

[52] The Economist podcast, *feeds.feedburner.com/economist/audio_all.*

[53] MommyCast podcast, *podcast.mommycast.com.*

[54] Whirlpool podcast, *www.whirlpool.com/custserv/promo. jsp?sectionId=563*

[55] General Electric podcast, www.ge.com/news/audio_video/audio_ podcast.html.

[56]   United Nations podcast, www.unfoundation.org/blog-multimedia/ podcasts.
[57]   World Health Organization podcast, *www.who.int/mediacentre/ multimedia/podcasts/en/index.html.*
[58]   Humane Society podcast, *video.hsus.org/*
[59]   International Olympic Committee podcast, *www.olympic.org/uk/news/ podcast/index_uk.asp.*
[60]   The Cullinane and Green Report, *cullinane-green.podomatic.com.*
[61]   White House Briefing Room, *www.whitehouse.gov/briefing_room.*
[62]   Paul Verna, "Video Content: Harnessing a Mass Audience," *eMarketer,* November 2008.
[63]   Donna Hoffman, "Managing Beyond Webb 2.0," *McKinsey Quarterly,* July 2009.
[64]   "Consumer Electronics Products and Services Usage Report,"*Accenture,* 2009.
[65]   David Hallerman, "Video Advertising Online: Spending and Pricing," *eMarketer,* September 2008.
[66]   Viddler, *www.viddler.com*
[67]   John Earnhardt, "Cisco CEO Challenge: Use Collaborative Technologies to Cut Back Travel," Cisco blog: *The Platform,* June 15, 2009.
[68]   The Humane Society, *www.hsus.org.*
[69]   Wayne Pacelle blog, *hsus.typepad.com.*
[70]   BlendTec, "Will It Blend," *YouTube Channel, www.youtube.com/user/ Blendtec.*
[71]   WebMD blog, *www.Webmd.com/community/blogs.*

Chapter 4

[72]   "The State of Search Engine Marketing 2006," *Search Engine Marketing Professional Organization (SEMPO),* January 2007.
[73]   "Why Search Matters to Local Business," *WebVisible,* 2007.
[74]   "The Power of Google is Self Evident," *Wall Street Journal,* June 10, 2009.
[75]   Google Custom Search, *www.google.com/coop/cse.*
[76]   Charles Knight AltSearchEngine Blog, *www.altsearchengines.com.*
[77]   Shopzilla, *www.shopzilla.com.*
[78]   DealTime, *www.dealtime.com.*
[79]   PriceScan, *www.pricescan.com.*

[80] David Felfoldi, "Search Engine Marketing: Outsource or In-House," *MarketingProfs.com,* August 7, 2007.

[81] Gail Kalinoski, "Case Study: Natural Search Program Boosts Pottery Barn's Online Traffic, Visibility, and Revenue," *All About Retail/Catalog Online Integration,* June 1, 2007.

[82] Wolfram Research, *www.wolframalpha.com.*

[83] "The State of Search Engine Marketing 2006," *Search Engine Marketing Professional Organization (SEMPO),* January 2007.

Chapter 5

[84] "Wave 3: Power to the People Social Media Tracker," *Universal McCann Study,* March, 2008.

[85] Danah Boyd, Nicole Ellison, "Social Network Sites: Definition, History, and Scholarship," *Journal of Computer-Mediated Communication,* 2007, 13(1).

[86] Mark Granovetter, "The Strength of Weak Ties," *An American Journal of Sociology,* May 1973, V78, N6, 1360-1338.

[87] "Wave 3: Power to the People Social Media Tracker," *Universal McCann Study,* March, 2008.

[88] LinkedIn About Us Web page, *press.linkedin.com/about.*

[89] Facebook Press Web page, *www.facebook.com/press/info.php?statistics.*

[90] Alexa Top Site Rankings, *www.alexa.com/topsites.*

[91] John Hagel, John Seely Brown, "Life on the Edge: Learning From Facebook," *Business Week,* April 2, 2008.

[92] "Just Under Half of Americans Have a Facebook or MySpace Account," *Harris Interactive,* April 16, 2009.

[93] "70% of Americans Aged 15-34 Use Social Networks," *The Womma Word: WOM You Need To Know,* May 11, 2007.

[94] "Wave 3: Power to the People Social Media Tracker," *Universal McCann Study,* March, 2008.

[95] Spencer E. Ante, Catherine Holahan, "Generation MySpace is Getting Fed Up," *Business Week,* February 2, 2008.

[96] Jeremiah Owyang, "Social Network Stats: Facebook, MySpace, Reunion (Jan, 2008)," *Web Strategy by Jeremiah Owyang,* January 9, 2008.

[97] Marc Cieslak, "Evolution of the Social Network," *BBC News,* March 28, 2009.

[98] Joan Voight, "Social Marketing Do's and Don'ts," *AdWeek,* October 8, 2007.

[99] Disney-Pixar on Facebook, *www.facebook.com/DisneyPixar.*

100 Verizon Wireless on Facebook, www.facebook.com/verizon.

101 Blockbuster on Facebook, *www.facebook.com/blockbuster.*

102 AT&T on Facebook, *www.facebook.com/ATT.*

103 Coca Cola on Facebook, *www.facebook.com/coca-cola.*

104 Carnival Cruise Line on Facebook, *www.facebook.com/Carnival.*

105 Proctor & Gamble on Facebook, *www.facebook.com/procterngamble.*

106 Where Are You Now, *www.wayn.com.*

107 Microsoft on Facebook, *www.facebook.com/Microsoft.*

108 Starbucks on Facebook, *www.facebook.com/Starbucks.*

109 Goldman Sachs Alumni Network, *www.gsalumninetwork.com.*

110 Deloitte Alumni Network, *www.alumni.deloitte.com.*

111 The Humane Society of the United States on Facebook, *www.facebook. com/humanesociety.*

112 The American Heart Association on Facebook, *www.facebook.com/Start WalkingNow.*

113 World Wide Life Fund on Facebook, *www.facebook.com/ worldwildlifefund.*

114 Oxfam International on Facebook, *www.facebook.com/oxfamamerica.*

115 Kiva on Facebook, *www.facebook.com/kiva.*

Chapter 6

116 James Surowiecki, "Smarter Than The CEO," *Wired,* June 2004.

117 Jeff Howe, *Crowdsourcing: Why the Power of the Crowd is Driving the Future of Business,* (New York: Crown Publishing, 2008).

118 Ellen McGirt, "How Cisco's CEO John Chambers is Turning the Tech Giant Socialist," *FastCompany.com,* November 3, 2008.

119 Webex, *www.Webex.com.*

120 Live Meeting, *www.livemeeting.com.*

121 Go To Meeting, *www.gotomeeting.com.*

122 Adobe Connect, *www.adobe.com/products/acrobatconnectpro.*

123 Stream57, *www.stream57.com.*

124 Skype, *www.skype.com.*

125 Gardiner Morse, "Wikipedia Founder Jimmy Wales on Making the Most of Company Wikis," *Harvard Business Review,* April 2008.

126 "SAP Fosters Collaboration and Education Among its Growing Business Process Expert Community," *SAP Press Release,* May 20, 2008.

127 J.R.R. Tolkien wiki, *en.wikipedia.org/wiki/J._R._R._Tolkien.*

128 Virtual Worlds Expo, *www.virtualworldsexpo.com.*

[129] "Innovation in Virtual Worlds," *IBM Research.*

[130] Erica Driver, Paul Jackson, "Getting Work Done in Virtual Worlds," *Forrester Research,* January 7, 2008.

[131] Jose Antonio Vargas, "Virtual Reality Prepares Soldiers for Real War," *The Washington Post,* February 24, 2006.

[132] "Virtual Heroes Help Duke University Create Interactive Healthcare Training Program," *Virtual Heroes News Room,* March 3, 208.

[133] "BreakAway Licenses Pulse!! Virtual Learning Platform for Medical Training," *Virtual World News Online,* May 7, 2008.

[134] Lisa LaMotta, "Trade Shows, Web 2.0 Style," *Forbes Magazine,* September 14, 2007.

Chapter 7

[135] Steve Hamm, "How Cloud Computing Will Change Business," *Business Week,* June 4, 2009.

[136] Philip Delves Broughton, "Ready for a Change," *Wall Street Journal Online,* May 21, 2009.

[137] Arnold Schwarzenegger, "Digital Textbook Can Save Money, Improve Learning," *Mercury News,* June 7, 2009.

[138] "Avatars That Look Like Us," *World Future Society,* June 2009, V10, N6.

Index

D

digital advertising tools, 19
Dorsey, Jack, 35
Dougherty, Dale, 22
Duke University, 86

E

Economist, 43
eMarketer, 42, 45, 47, 69

F

"first mover," 15
Forester Research, 85
   "Getting Work Done in Virtual
      Worlds," 85
Future Arrived Yesterday, The (Malone),
   93

G

General Electric, 36, 44
Generation Y, 14
"Getting Work Done in Virtual
      Worlds" (Forester Research), 85
Global Positioning System technology,
   17, 92
Godin, Seth, 32
Google, 23, 53–55, 57
GPS. *See* Global Positioning System
   technology

H

Hamm, Steve, 92
Harvard Business Review, 80
Hoffman, Donna, 46
Howe, Jeff, 78, 106
   Crowdsourcing, 78

Humane Society of the United States,
   47
   Animal Channel, 47

I

IBM, 84–85
Internet, 22, 78, 91
   number of people with access to, 19
   usage, 19, 21
Internet video, 45, 48
   growth in, 45
interruption marketing, 18, 90
   factors that weaken, 20
      annoyance factor, 21
      attention span, 21
      emergence of online communities,
         21
      eroding trust, 21
      irrelevance, 20
      new technologies and legislation,
         21
      overexposure, 20
iPhone, 48, 92
iTunes, 41–42

J

Jetblue Airways Corporation, 22
Johns Hopkins University, 86
Johnson, Steven, 35

K

Kawasaki, Guy, 32, 36
   "Looking for Mr. Goodtweet: How
      to Pick Up Followers on Twitter,"
      32, 36, 102–3
Kiva, 73
Knight, Charles, 55

Wikipedia, 81–82
Williams, Evan, 35
World Future Society, 94
World Wild Life Fund, 73

Y

Yahoo! 23, 53–54
Yankelovich Partners study, 20

Z

Zappos, 36

Edwards Brothers,Inc!
Thorofare, NJ 08086
19 January, 2011
BA2011019